ORACLE OF THE AGES

Pat Moore

Outside the log cabin home of the Lancaster family.

"The Oracle of the Ages" is the term that the late Amanda Mayhayley Lancaster, a nationally known psychic from Heard County, Georgia, often used to describe herself. But she was so much more than that. From the moment of her birth in October of 1875, when she came into the world wearing a caul, she began to make her mark on this rural corner of the Southeast, a mark that extended far beyond the boundaries of her county, her state, and her sociological status.

Home of the Lancaster Family from 1858 to 1952. Visitors seeking an audience with Mayhayley waited on the porch or stood in the yard among the dogs and cats and her lard buckets filled with flowers.

Superstition has it that those born with a caul, a membrane of skin that covers an infant's face at birth, have second sight. In Mayhayley's case, this seems to be true. She began telling fortunes at the age of six and continued, literally, until two days before her death in 1955. Mayhayley's remarkable psychic powers garnered national attention and helped her amass a small fortune despite her poor beginnings and humble living environment.

Mayhayley with her class at Red Oak School, Heard County, 1897.

The story of "Mayhayley, the Psychic" alone is worth retelling. But Mayhayley was much more than a celebrated seer. She was a driven woman who tried her hand at farming, law, real estate, gambling, politics, and much more — all unusual pursuits for a woman of her era. She also was a confounding, unpredictable woman who was both loved and hated by her family, friends, neighbors, and clients. She had astonishing looks—a tall, rail-thin, almost masculine figure and an empty eye socket that she sometimes filled with an ordinary marble.

The Lancaster family, photographed in front of their house, 1904.

She dressed in extreme fashions, from garish feathers and beads to flour sacks and tire-tread shoes.

This book portrays this remarkable, enigmatic woman by viewing her myriad sides through the eyes of people who knew her. It is an attempt to tell her story with historical and factual accuracy while also bringing to life the people and community in which she lived.

— RICKIE BRUNER, ARCHIVIST, ALABAMA
DEPARTMENT OF ARCHIVES AND HISTORY

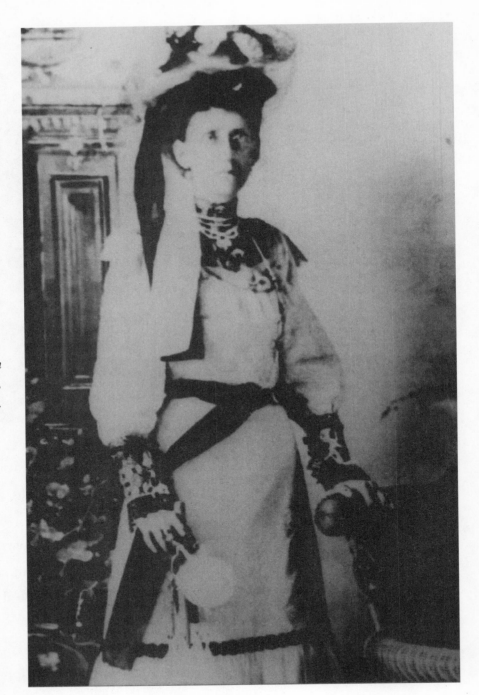

Mayhayley in her twenties, about 1904.

Mayhayley,
mid-1920s.

Mayhayley used this photograph in her September 1922, campaign for the Georgia Senate. She is thought to be the first woman to seek public office in the State of Georgia. Inset below, a photo from her 1928 campaign for the same office.

*Mayhayley
with her "law
books."*

*A sample of
Mayhayley's
handwriting.*

ORACLE OF THE AGES

REFLECTIONS ON THE CURIOUS LIFE
OF FORTUNE TELLER MAYHAYLEY LANCASTER

DOT MOORE
WITH KATIE LAMAR SMITH

NewSouth Books
Montgomery

NewSouth Books
P.O. Box 1588
Montgomery, AL 36102

This book is a work of creative non-fiction. The names, places, and
incidents are real and grounded in extensive research. Some dialogue
between characters was created to advance the story.

Library of Congress Cataloging-in-Publication Data
Moore, Dot, 1931-
Oracle of the ages : reflections on the curious life of fortune teller
Mayhayley Lancaster / Dot Moore with Katie Lamar Smith
p. cm.
includes bibliographical references (p.) and index.
ISBN 1-58838-007-6
1. Lancaster, Mayhayley, 1874-1955. 2. Fortune-tellers—Georgia—
Heard County—Biography. I. Smith, Katie Lamar. II. Title
BF1815.L36 M66 2001
133.3'092—dc21
[B]
200104429

Design by Randall Williams
Printed in the United States of America
by Phoenix Color Corporation

SECOND PRINTING

Sources of Photographs:
Pages 2–3, L. F. Simpkins; 4, Heard County Historical Society; 5, Del
Kuhlman; 6, Barbara Yates Hohl; 7, Mack and Barbara Mitchell; 8,
Lillian Smith Davis and Heard County Historical Society; 9, Del
Kuhlman; 10, Barbara Yates Hohl; 58–59, J. C. Otwell; 74, Dell
Publications and J. C. Otwell; 112, Keneth Roberts and L. F.
Simpkins; 113, Del Kuhlman; 160, *Atlanta Constitution*.

TO MY CHILDREN
LAURA, MARJORIE, RUSSELL, AND WILL
AND THEIR SPOUSES
MIKE, ALEX, DANA, AND MANDY

AND TO MY GRANDCHILDREN
AND IN LOVING MEMORY OF SCOTTIE

ALSO TO THE PEOPLE OF HEARD COUNTY, GEORGIA,
LIVING AND DEAD,
WHO BELIEVED IN MAYHAYLEY AND IN ME!

Contents

PROLOGUE: FIRST SIGHT · 17

ACKNOWLEDGMENTS · 23

1 · THROUGH THE EYES OF A CHILD · 27

2 · THE EYES OF THE LAW · 44

3 · A CRITIC'S EYE · 60

4 · EYES IN CRAWFISHES' TAILS · 75

5 · THE PREACHER'S WIFE SEES IT ALL · 86

6 · EXAMINING THE SKELETONS IN THE CLOSET · 101

7 · HINDSIGHT · 114

8 · EVIE SEES IT DIFFERENTLY · 128

EPILOGUE: LAST SIGHT · 140

APPENDICES:

CHRONOLOGY · 143

TRANSCRIPT OF WALLACE TRIAL TESTIMONY · 147

WILL OF MAYHAYLEY LANCASTER · 155

INDEX · 157

Prologue

First Sight

I HEARD MAYHAYLEY BEFORE I SAW HER. SHE WAS TALKING LOUDLY TO HER companion, another woman near her age. Reflection indicates it was probably her sister, Sallie. As the two moved between the headstones over the clean-swept ground among the graves, Mayhayley was interrupting the conversations of others with calls and greetings to tightly knotted family groups who stood among the graves of their family members. The "others" in the cemetery were probably church members who had come the day before and cleaned off the graveyard, wrestling with year-old weeds and spreading white sand on unmarked graves. Visitors such as us only brought florist shop flowers for the graves and home-cooked food for "dinner on the grounds."

Heard County folks always stand respectfully and quietly by their family graves (even today, this is so), which Mayhayley surely knew because she was more than sixty years old and had gone to Decoration Day services at the church all her life. Nevertheless, her clatter announced her coming.

I turned to see her. She was a tall, skinny-looking woman wearing layers of dresses with long voluminous skirts that swung as she walked. Tied about a waistcoat of some kind were ribbons, cords, and belts. A multitude of necklaces jangled around her neck, and on her head was a bright red hat that sported flowers, feathers, and beads threaded into its crown. She was carrying a fan, a ledger book, and a Bible in one hand. As I was to learn later, Mayhayley always carried something to read. In the other hand, she clutched some flowers along with her purse—a colorful cloth sack that perhaps once held flour.

Her face was heavily wrinkled, old. This day being a Sunday, she wore rouge and yellow face powder, a luxury for most Heard County women, and reserved for Sundays.

It is the eyes I remember best. Her right eye was brown and well-shaped, but her left eye sank deep into the recesses of her face. From that indentation came a glinting, flashing light as she turned her head from side to side in that bright sun. While the artificial glass eye frightened some children, I do not remember being afraid.

That was the first time I remember seeing Mayhayley Lancaster. We were at Macedonia Baptist Church graveyard in May of 1937. I was a little girl nearly six years old, standing with my daddy, my two older brothers, and other kinfolk—maybe ten or twelve in all—at the grave of my mother.

On that Decoration Day our immediate family had traveled the thirty or so miles north from our home in LaGrange to Heard County, then westward to the place where my mother's funeral had been held the previous fall in the white, country church beside the graveyard.

I think I liked Mayhayley, beginning just then, as she approached our group. She was smiling, sort of chuckling, and still waving her long arm to others as she neared our family group. I think my daddy was smiling, too. Maybe he was flattered that she chose our group to join. Looking back, it seems to me that there was a mutual admiration between the two—perhaps a respect that each shared for the other's talents. I would not say that I fell in love with her, as children are sometimes inclined to do when they see a celebrity, particularly one as colorful as Mayhayley, but I confess that she affected me that day and has shadowed me ever since.

Amanda Mayhayley Lancaster was born in Heard County, Georgia, on October 18, 1875, the third of eleven children begotten to Harriet and John Lancaster. Her birth was unusual, according to neighbors and her family. Most agree that she came into the world wearing a caul, a thin layer of membrane that covered her face. This, according to obstetricians and midwives, happens sometimes when the placental sack remains attached to the baby's body as it passes through the birth canal. It is unusual, but not abnormal. In many cultures, however, those born with the caul (also called a veil, a mask, or a double veil) are often thought to have special powers—given second sight, some say. Charles Dickens said in *David Copperfield*, which is believed to be autobiographical, "I was born with a caul" and reminded his readers that a caul was a valuable article and lent special favors. In Mayhayley's case, that seemed to be true.

She began telling fortunes when she was six and was still telling them when she died at the age of seventy-nine. Fortune telling made Mayhayley famous and helped her amass a great deal of wealth. Yet, in the years between her unusual birth and her death, she did much more than tell fortunes. She was a schoolteacher (she taught my grandmother), a door-to-door saleswoman, a newspaper reporter, a successful businesswoman, and an unsuccessful farmer. She practiced law (whether she did so with the benefit of a degree or certification is unclear) and ran for public office on what was, for her generation (and for many may still seem), a strikingly liberal and reformist platform. Mayhayley also dabbled along the edge of illegal gambling while at the same time she served as an informant for law officials in her area and throughout the South.

Even if these many varied vocations and avocations had not been curious for a woman of her times, Mayhayley's appearance would have set her apart from her world. She was taller than most women—probably five feet, ten inches—and gaunt. She had high cheekbones and the swarthy complexion of the Welsh people. Her nose and chin were sharp, thin, and hawkish. She walked in long, masculine strides—some people thought she looked more like a man than a woman.

Her fashion sense was unusual and prone to extremes. There were times in her life when she dressed garishly, bedecked with brightly colored clothes and hats, feather boas and ribbons and jewelry. She wore Victorian-style, high-topped shoes. At other times in her life, she wore plain, ill-fitted dresses covered with soiled aprons and feed sacks tied to her rail-thin body with ropes and/or wires. In her later years, she was often seen wearing a faded sunbonnet or a moth-eaten old Army hat of uncertain origin. "When she was poor, she dressed rich; when she was rich, she dressed poor," someone once said to me.

Among the peculiar and often shocking aspects of her appearance was the absence of her left eye and its demise still remains a mystery. Stories abound about how she actually lost it; though no one seems to know the real truth. Sometimes, she would leave the eye socket empty or cover it with a pirate's patch. Other times she would fill the empty void with a marble embellished with a hand-painted iris and red, bloodshot lines, or she might just wear a regular marble of whatever fractured shade and color was available. Almost always, the eye oozed a rheumy fluid that ran down her cheek.

She never married nor to my knowledge, ever had a lover. In fact, the only real love of her life appears to have been her younger sister, Sallie, who was likely with her that first day I saw her. She also loved money and attention. She could be kind and generous with her psychic talents but was also penurious, and she could be cruel and abusive to people she did not like. She cursed and prayed with equal fervor and abandon (a trait common among southerners). She abhorred drinking and flirtatious girls, yet seemed to have no problem with gamblers and whiskey runners.

Mayhayley was an enigma to all: those who knew her well (including her family) and those who knew of her (including myself). This should not convey that Mayhayley consumed my life from that first day forward. It was nearly forty years later that I truly began to let Mayhayley into my life. During those four decades between our initial meeting and my first attempts to learn more about Mayhayley, I went on with my life, living it quite separately from hers. I reared four children on my own following the untimely death of my husband, Joe. I was (and still remain) active in the Democratic Party, taught school, worked as a writer for the State Department of Post Secondary Education, and sated my interest in human rights and civil rights by working within my community for causes I felt compelled to further. All those endeavors engaged me more than Mayhayley for much of my life.

Yet, my interest in her grew so much through the years, that, in 1976, I began to investigate her in earnest. My curiosity about Mayhayley turned to fascination as I unearthed information about her that revealed a life more perplexing than clear. My goal was to be her biographer, to get to know her and to understand her. Much of it, I did by interviewing the people of Heard County and surrounding areas who had known her personally. In the process, my research revealed as much, if not more, about a corner of the Deep South, its land and its people, as about Mayhayley. Partly because this was a place I loved, I kept digging.

Two years into my research, I fully realized that this was a complicated woman. The more I knew about her, the less I understood her. It occurred to me to investigate Mayhayley's roots, because I decided that if I knew her family, I would know Mayhayley better. My instincts must have been correct because I immediately received what must have been a "sign." When I first entered the library of the Alabama Department of Archives and History in Montgomery, Alabama, I took my place at a table where some previous browser or excavator had left a single book. It was a copy of the directory to the 1820 Georgia Census. I flipped open the cover to the index where my eyes immediately focused on one name — Lancaster, Mahala. Could it be, I muttered aloud, that accidentally or providentially, I had discovered Mayhayley herself or an ancestors of hers? Perhaps it was a great, great-grandmother? Within minutes, I had uncovered what could have represented many years of digging. My quest was in earnest and I had gotten some help from Someone.

During the time, energy, and expense that followed I joyfully learned about Mayhayley. I still do not completely understand her, but I am content to wait for understanding to come. I cannot even fully answer the question, "Why do I care about Mayhayley?" I may never answer that question, but I suspect it is because she lived creatively, cut her own path undaunted by social convention, and was one firmly in the world but not a product of it. I liked her politics, which disclosed her desire to perform, if given the chance, as a true public servant. Neither racism and sexism nor lust for power informed her mind over those who differed. She was Difference Defined.

She was a rugged, unbecoming agrarian woman who, despite her physical and societal limitations, became a national celebrity, hosting people from all walks of life, and from great distances, in her ramshackle house. Many people—even those who did not believe in her powers of prophecy—described her as brilliant, smarter than most, and she was highly respected by most of her native people. Yet, there was also the less laudable side of Mayhayley. She could be avaricious and, consequently, made no attempt to economically better her community. For all the reported wealth she amassed its residue attests to some tasteless, tawdry, wasteful mark upon this earth. A broken grave is her only tangible gift.

Human beings are complicated creatures, and the human condition constitutes both good and bad traits in each individual body and soul. Yet few were as tangled as Mayhayley Lancaster.

My research illustrated that to even try to understand this complicated woman, we must look at her through many eyes and minds. This book attempts to capture the complicated essence of Amanda Mayhayley Lancaster through the eyes and views of others: her young neighbor, Willis Hemmings; highway patrolman, J. C. Otwell; dramatist, Hettie Jane Dunaway Sewell; convicted murderer, John Wallace; the local Baptist preacher's wife, Clara Heard Bryan; Mayhayley's sister, Mary: attorney Frank Gearreld; and her sister Sallie's daughter-in-law: Evie Farmer Mitchell—whose lives, like mine, became entangled with hers.

Acknowledgments

THE BOOK BEGAN AS AN IDEA OF MINE AND MY COUSIN DOCK HEARD Davis, his daddy, my uncle, Owen Davis, and a special friend, Carolyn Clarke. We began the book on a dark day in a pouring down rain on December 11, 1976, by first visiting Evie Mitchell and then Luther Wyatt. Then we rented a Franklin post office box to receive the letters we were sure would result from a newspaper ad requesting Mayhayley stories. Our plan was that those letters would comprise the book. There would be hundreds of letters, we thought, and they would make up the book. After a month of notices in the Heard County newspaper, we received four.

One of the letters was from J. C. Otwell, the state trooper who "took the money to the bank" and therein began the wonderful journey up and down the roads of Heard, Carroll, Coweta, Meriwether and Troup County, Georgia. There were also interviews in Randolph, Cleburne, Walker and Chambers County, Alabama.

The book would not have been possible without the support of Judge Lamar Knight of Carrollton, Georgia, Mayhayley's attorney who had grown up at the Caney Head Church community in Heard County and had known her as a child.

Of course, the core of the book is made from those many persons who were willing to be interviewed. And how could I have endured the years of research without my Heard cousins who knew Mayhayley far better than I! They contributed the food, the fun, the fellowship and the housing; especially Dock Heard Davis and Janie and their children, Rebecca Jane Davis Lawley and Joe and their children,

23

Doyle and Margaret Garrett and their children, Randy and Shirley Garrett, Nelva and David Roop, and my mother's only living sister, Jimmie Mae Heard Arrington-Kuglar. And, of course, my own two brothers, Blake and Johnson, and Lillian, my daddy's pretty wife.

Katie Lamar Smith was and is EVERYTHING to me and to the book. The layout of the book was her idea and the characterizations were further developed by her. The day I met her at the Auburn Public Library at one of my "Tales of Mayhayley" storyfests was my lucky day! And Mayhayley's!

The following contributed their stories or their know-how to this creative non-fiction biography of Miss Amanda Mayhayley Lancaster (1875-1955.) They were interviewed, both formally and informally, over many years. Some talked with me many times; others, only briefly. Many of the interviews, and in no certain order, were recorded and all were dated: Willis Hemmings, Frank Gearreld, Clara Heard Bryan, J.C. Otwell, Celestine Sibley, Frank Parks, Evie Farmer Mitchell, Luther Wyatt, Lamar Knight, James Bryan, Doris Owensby, Wheeler Bryan, Lela Ridley Persons, Reverend Herman Caldwell, Render Caswell, Dr. Doyle Caswell, Elmer Garrett, J.R. Garrett, Jimmie Mae Heard Kuglar, Owen Cook Davis, Senior, Dr. James Bryant, Mrs. Earl Adams, Linda Eller, Howard Kinney, Selmah Bowen, Clark Johnson, Dock Heard Davis, Reuben Word, Blake Edward Davis, Lillian Smith Davis, Johnson Edmond Davis, Mary Smith Ellenburg, Nellie Shaddix, Nancy Ann Davis, Barbara Yates Hohl, Doyle Garrett, Steve Lipford, Wright Lipford, Mort Lipford, Thomas Lipford, Louise Sledge, Annie Wallace, Winnie Davis Stephens, Ben R. Hyatt, Ambrose Spradlin, Esta Davis Gore, Louise Gore, Frank Gore, Glovis Gore, Tom Sellers, Barry Lancaster, O.D. Janney, Rebecca Jane Davis Lawley, Bill Slay, Holland Ware, Del Kuhlman, Tommie Cosper McCutcheon, Lunie Bledsoe, Herschel Bryan, Bill Yearch, Walter Skinner, Marvin Noles, Grover Lancaster, Watson Lancaster, John L. Heard, Pat Glover, Thomas Glover, Bobby Hammond, Coy Trammel Hudson, Minnie Ann Louvorn, Ted Barker, James Eddie Barker, Virgina Aldridge, CarolineWest, Mickey Noles, Caroline Yates Abercrombie, Bobby Stewart, Jenny Futral, Mary Faver, Mavis Thompson, Mary Lou Thaxton, Reuben Thaxton, Thomas Stutts, Sheriff Virgil

Bledsoe, Carl Simonton, Randy Allen, Doris Wilkinson, Lena Latimer Murphy, Jonathan Lancaster, Willie Phillips, Ray Brown, Alfred Zachry, James C. Bonner, Beulah Daniel, Dr. Thomas Reeve, Jr., Ferroll Sams, James Mitchell, and many others who stopped me on the street just to tell their story!!

Thanks to those who provided the Photographs: Del Kuhlman, J. C. Otwell, Mary Lancaster Arrington, Barbara Yates Hohl, Barbara and Mackey Mitchell, Kenneth Roberts, L.F. Simkins, and Lillian Smith Davis as well as the Heard County Historical Center and Museum, the Heard County Historical Society, the Newnan, Georgia, *Times-Herald,* the Franklin, Georgia, *News and Banner,* the LaGrange, Georgia, *Daily News,* the University of Georgia Archives, the Atlanta *Constitution,* the *Atlanta Journal,* and the *Columbus Ledger.*

On-going support of the project came from my friends Jessie and Carl Summers, Jr., of the Chattahoochee Valley Historical Society and the Lee County Historical Society.

Professional help has been given by Granger Carr, writer; Dr. Judith Paterson, journalism professor and author; Guy Martin, writer; Max Adams, architect and grammarian; Gillis Morgan, journalism professor and newspaper editor; Rickie Bruner, archivist; Thomas Bobo, author of children's books; John Wagnon, painter of Mayhayley's portrait; and especially, Forrest Clark Johnson, III, historian and history teacher, and Winston Skinner, reporter and assistant news editor for the *Times-Herald,* Newnan, Georgia.

How could we get our local history without the hard volunteer work of members of our historical societies? And those who have established museums and archives in West Georgia have given me the most help of all; especially the Troup County, Georgia Historical Society and Archives, Kaye Minchew, director; the Harris County Historical Society, the Chattahoochee Valley Alabama Historical Society, the Lee County Alabama Historical Society, the Coweta County, Georgia Male Museum, Jo Anne Ray, then-director, The Carroll County Historical Society, and the Heard County Georgia Historical Society, especially Lela Craft, Selmah Bowen and Rebecca Lawley.

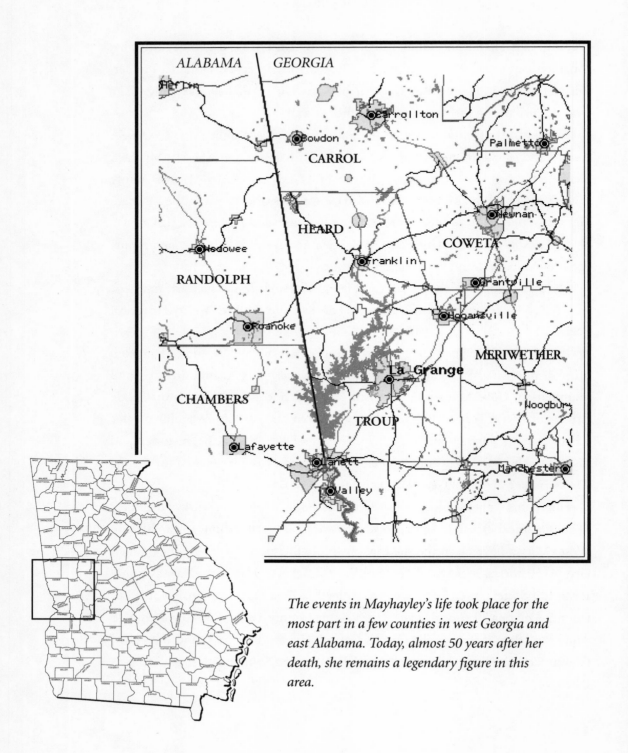

The events in Mayhayley's life took place for the most part in a few counties in west Georgia and east Alabama. Today, almost 50 years after her death, she remains a legendary figure in this area.

1

Through the Eyes of a Child

WILLIS HEMMINGS AND HIS FAMILY HAD MOVED AROUND SHARE-cropping FOR most of his young life. He could not remember exactly how old he was when they settled into the old, unpainted, dog-trot house up the road from Mayhayley. He just remembered what it was like coming to their own house with its four rooms, two on each side of the "trot" and its slanting front porch that tilted toward a bare, treeless front yard. He remembered that he had learned quickly not to shuffle his bare feet across the floors unless he wanted to get splinters. He also remembered how cold it was when they first moved in, right after Christmas when a winter draft blew constantly through the rooms.

Despite all these problems, the house was new to them and it was a permanent place to live. It was also where Willis discovered Mayhayley, or, maybe, she discovered him. They had spent the holiday with Willis's grandmother—his father's mother—on their way to Heard County, where they hoped to start a fresh life after having a bad experience working on thirds and fourths over in Alabama. Willis was glad to get there. He would be glad about Mayhayley, too.

When they rented the house from John Bledsoe, they unpacked their few possessions: a change of clothes, some cooking utensils, and a few sticks of cast-off furniture. They immediately got to work stuffing newspapers in the walls' cracks, cleaning out the fireplace, and oiling the rusty hinges so that when spring came they could open a window. The best part of Willis's young life was when his mother lighted the kerosene lamp and read Bible verses to him and his brothers and sister. It was the only book they had. She also read the old newspapers that were left over from the wall-stuffing.

Willis was a good kid and a hard worker. Though small for his age, he was wiry, strong and quick. He could chase a chicken down, chop its head off, and drop it in a pot of hot water to loosen its feathers, quick as a lick. After his mother cut up the chicken and cooked it in lard, he was happy to take a wing, a back, or the neck for all his work. He could chop wood for the open fireplace and for his mother's wood cook stove, and he would bring the wood into the house and stack it neatly. He drew water from a well, and, small as he was, he could milk a cow. Of course he could drop cottonseeds into hard, lumpy soil, too. When he got older, he would learn to use the long-handled hoe to chop cotton (clean out the weeds) and at harvest time he would drag a heavy, burlap sack filled with cotton back to their house, just like his older brothers.

One night at supper, in 1934, Willis's father mentioned that a neighbor-woman had stopped by to tell him that she was hoping to get electricity and they might be getting it, too, in a year or two. That was all that his father said about the woman. A few days later Mr. Bledsoe came by in his car and announced that Rural Electric would be coming around sometime and that they'd be wiring houses for "the juice." He would see that they had electricity if they thought they could pay the monthly bill which, he thought, would range from seventy-five cents to a $1.25 a month, depending on how careful they were. While his father had no idea how he would come up with the money, he optimistically said that, yes, they would manage somehow and he hoped that Mr. Bledsoe would sign up the house. In later years Willis's father often said that the day he switched on the lights was the happiest day of his life!

Time passed and it was getting warmer, probably late March, and Willis was helping his mother sort out seeds for a vegetable garden. She had dried them and put them in fruit jars the year before and brought them with her from Alabama. She planned to get them out when the ground got warm and when the moon was just right, she told Willis.

They were sitting out on the front porch and his mother was telling him about weather signs when they saw two women walking up the road toward their house. His mother was hopeful that they were coming to visit her and in a way they were.

Both women were tall and slender. They were wearing typical farm-women attire: cloth dresses made from flour sacks, matching sun bonnets, and men's brogan shoes. Each one carried a shoebox that she extended from her arms as if making an offering. They were not talking to one another as they seriously approached Mrs. Hemmings and Willis.

When they came into the yard and approached the porch, Willis could see them clearly and was fascinated by the pair. One, the smaller of the two, was rather pretty. The other was gangly and almost masculine, and it was obvious something was wrong with her left eye. He could not take his eyes off her as she politely asked his mother, "Are you the lady of the house?"

When Mrs. Hemmings replied that she was, except that her husband was in the field if they needed to talk business, the taller one introduced herself. "I'm your neighbor, Mayhayley Lancaster, and this is my sister, Sallie." Then she began a speech that seemed to have been prepared. She was selling vegetable and flower seeds, she said, and they were ready to be planted now. If Willis's mother would like to buy some seeds, she would guarantee them to be the very best seeds on the market. The woman went on to tell them that she used these very seeds and she had won contests in the produce competition every year at Carrollton A&M (first called Fourth District Agricultural and Mechanical School) since 1908, when the school started. The seeds were only ten cents a package, she said, and each package had a pretty picture on the front and written instructions on the backside.

Because Willis and his mother were coincidentally counting and examining seeds, they were very interested. They had no seeds for squash, so Mrs. Hemmings quickly said that yes, she would buy the squash seeds, that is, if she could find the money. She had not counted her "egg money" since they moved in, but she was sure that there was a little money left in her handbag. Excusing herself, she went into the house and soon returned with the dime. Willis sat still, looking at the women and feeling in awe of Mayhayley.

"You can take my word. When you plant these seeds you'll get squash as big as a twenty-pound lard bucket. If I'm wrong, you come on down to my house and I'll make it up to you," Mayhayley declared.

When she said "down to my house" she pointed across the road and down the trail that Willis had already thought about exploring, if and when his chores allowed.

The women went on their way.

During the next week, Willis went down the road to Mayhayley's log cabin and told Mayhayley that they had planted the squash seeds and they sure hoped they would work out just fine. This polite remark endeared Willis to Mayhayley and they became even faster friends when he offered his services to her. Yes, he said, he could do anything and he would not ask for much money. "Just what you can spare," he said. Willis had no idea that, by their standards, Mayhayley was a very rich woman. He certainly could not tell it from the condition of her hewn log cabin house.

"Could you climb up on the roof and stop the leaking?" she asked the child.

Not knowing what he was in for, Willis looked in the barn and found an old wooden ladder that was lying among rusted, broken plows and plowshares. By himself, he dragged the ladder to the front of her house and, with the help of some men who seemed to be standing around, they leaned the ladder against the roof, where it stayed until 1952 when the log house burned. When the ladder was in place, little Willis carefully climbed up its loose rungs and saw that the shakes and shingles were either broken or missing. He climbed down and searched for some fieldstones that were small enough for him to tote back up the ladder and put in the places of the missing wooden shingles. All day, back and forth, the little fellow crawled up and down the ladder repairing Mayhayley's roof.

When he was bone tired and had used every reasonable rock he could find, Willis reported back to Mayhayley. She ceremoniously rewarded him with a dime. While the money was far too little for his efforts, it was the first money Willis ever had. It was then that he decided to come back every chance he got, and he calculated on his way home that he could make seventy cents a week, at a dime a day!

He was correct. He brought in Mayhayley's wood, swept off her creaky front porch, and helped her plant her seeds with the pretty pictures on the packages. She planted flowers: marigolds, zinnias, and nasturtiums. She also had some dahlia cuttings, which he helped her put in one of many rusty lard buckets that were spread throughout her yard.

"Why don't you plant them in the ground as we do, Miss Mayhayley?" Willis asked.

"And let the goddamned dogs dig them up?" she replied.

Willis had never heard a woman use words that only men used when they were out of earshot of women. He soon learned that Mayhayley said lots of curse words. She sometimes used the bad words when she was angry and sometimes she used the words when she was telling Willis a story. She was a good storyteller, but she did not seem to like to answer his questions and even though Willis was mighty interested in how she lost her eye, he never asked. He figured it got infected and a doctor took it out, which turned out to be close to what Mayhayley once said in her weekly newspaper column.

Soon, Willis was at Mayhayley's house whenever he was able to rush through his own work. His parents were glad to see the extra money come into the house for it was more than was needed to pay for the electricity, the only luxury they had.

When the squash plants blossomed, they produced the largest flowers Willis and his parents had ever seen. Their other summer vegetables were puny and small compared to the squash, which continued to grow and grow until the fruits were comfortably heavy to carry into the house for cooking. Willis hauled a squash to Mayhayley and Sallie.

"Willis," Mayhayley said, "go get me an empty lard bucket from behind the chicken house." When he returned, she had him pick up the squash and lay it on the top of the twenty-pound lard bucket. It rested easy. From that day forward, Willis and his family believed fully in Mayhayley.

When fall came, all the Hemmings went to the field to pick cotton. At dusk they returned with the day's largess and emptied the sacks on the floor of the open-ended hall, the dog-trot. When the hall was full, except for a narrow passageway to the four rooms, they began dumping their sacks on the front porch, for they had neither cotton shed nor any outbuildings. Mr. Hemmings was beginning to believe that their luck was changing and, like the squash, they would soon have a bountiful harvest in this their first year at the Bledsoe Place.

As the cotton was being heaved onto the front porch, the piles did not appear to grow; rather, each morning when Willis's father went out to look at the mounds of cotton they seemed to be the same size as the day before, or even smaller. They continued to pick the cotton and spread it on the porch. There was no way to explain the missing cotton.

Finally, Mr. Hemmings went to see Mayhayley. By then, they knew she was a fortune teller, though none of them had requested her services before.

When he explained his problem, Mayhayley appeared to be at a loss to understand what was happening. He told her again, that he, his wife, Willis, and the other children went out every morning at daylight and picked all day, stopping only to eat the food they carried out from their kitchen. When sundown came, they returned to the house and dumped their cotton on the porch. As hard as times were, he had earlier believed that they would have a good harvest and make some money, but now he was certain that something was happening to his cotton overnight.

"Does cotton shrink in the coolness of the evening in Heard County?" he inquired.

Mayhayley laughed out, but realizing the seriousness of his problem, she sat up straight and looked at him, concentrating so intensely that she appeared to be in consultation with herself. Finally she asked him some personal questions. Where did they first farm? Why did they leave Alabama? Did they have any plans for little Willis? What members of his family lived nearby?

He answered the questions, lastly telling her about his mother, his dead father, his sister, and his brothers, one of whom lived outside of Birmingham and worked at an ore mine. That was all. Unlike his wife's family, his was small, he explained.

Unable to give him a specific answer to the whereabouts of the cotton, she told him to go home and sit inside at night by the opening to the dog-trot so he could reach the switch to the light that swung from the rafter on the front porch.

"Someone is stealing your cotton," she said. "He will come back. If you will stay awake, you'll hear him. When the thief gets on your porch," she told him, "switch on the light. You'll know him," she prophesied. Then she instructed Mr. Hemmings to come back and tell her who it was because she had thought for a long time that somebody was stealing her cotton, too.

He did as she said.

After working all day, he sent his family off to bed at their regular bedtime and then he pulled up a chair at the door and sat in the darkness and watched and listened.

It was nearly midnight when he heard a soft, humming noise. It was the sound of a car slowly creeping up the road. Because there were no lights on or in the car, he could barely see the outline of a small automobile. Then he heard some faint noises, probably the sound of a car door opening or the car trunk being opened. He was not certain what he was hearing until he heard footfalls on the porch floor. It was then that he softly stood up, reached for the wall switch, and quickly flipped it. The porch was instantly bathed in stark, bright light. Mr. Hemmings looked into the face of the astonished prowler. It was a member of his own family.

The intruder jumped off the porch and raced to his car, which was still running. He floored the gas pedal and lit off from the Hemmings' yard with hard dirt and rocks flying through the air, some landing on their front porch.

Mr. Hemmings did not go back and tell Mayhayley who was getting his cotton. He was too ashamed. In fact, it was many years later before he told his wife and his by then adult son, Willis. Still, Mayhayley's advice put a stop to the cotton stealing, and Mr. Hemmings thought the squash seeds were some kind of a magic that got them off to a better start. Maybe the squash was voodoo, he once said, but, if so, it was good voodoo.

The next summer, on a late afternoon when everyone, including Sallie, was gone from Mayhayley's house, Willis was resting on her front porch and killing flies with his mother's fly swatter because Mayhayley could not find hers. He was sitting alone listening to rattling noises coming from the kitchen where Mayhayley was probably cooking her supper: a corn pone fried in hog grease, turnip greens that someone had canned the fall before, and some fried fat back — her usual fare.

The rattling stopped. Then he heard Mayhayley's shoes clomping down the hall toward him. He looked up at her when she opened the door and came out and sat beside him on the bench. She was smiling broadly and then she began to chuckle to herself.

The chuckling evolved into hearty, loud laughter. Mayhayley grabbed her own flat stomach and her body began to lurch back and forth as she continued laughing. When the laughter subsided a bit, Willis, who was now giggling himself, asked, "Miss Mayhayley what's so funny? Why are you laughing out so hard?"

Through her continued laughter, she gasped, "Oh, Willis, I just saw the funniest thing. It was the funniest thing I ever saw in my whole life! Oh, it was the funniest thing!"

Willis knew that she was alone in her house. He could not imagine what she could have seen, so he asked, "Miss Mayhayley, what did you see in the kitchen that was so funny?"

She continued to laugh and Willis sat and waited.

"Oh, Willis," she finally said, " I just saw God."

"God?" he exclaimed. "You saw God?"

Mayhayley continued, "I just saw God Almighty. He was standing out in the road and I saw Him pick up this pile of mule manure and roll it and roll it until He got this big turd, then, he leaned way back and slung this turd as hard as he could! It roared down the road, right up off of the ground, and it didn't stop till it killed seven preachers!"

Mayhayley's uproarious laughter now settled into a chuckle as she stood up, wiped her hands on her dress, and walked to the loose door frame. Without another word, she went through the door, letting the door slam haphazardly behind her and returned to the kitchen, still chuckling.

That was the only time she mentioned God to Willis, except to use God's name in vain, and she did that a lot.

The next summer one of Willis's girl cousins came to stay for two weeks with the Hemmings, a practice of most city families who had country relatives. While there, she was expected to help out, mind her aunt and uncle, and attend any revivals that were being held in the county. During the Depression, visiting kinfolk was the way poor children spent their summers. There was an added attraction for children who visited Heard County relatives in the summer. They got to go see Mayhayley.

Willis took his cousin, soon after she arrived, to see Mayhayley, and because they lived so close to her and she was so intrigued by her, the girl began to walk down to Mayhayley's cabin almost every afternoon.

One Sunday, a big, boisterous crowd was milling around in Mayhayley's yard when she got there. They were fun to watch, so, after slinking through the grownups and eyeing the children who were jumping on Mayhayley's bales of rotting cotton, she found an old tree stump on the far side of Mayhayley's house and sat down to watch some more.

She rubbed her bare feet back and forth in the sandy loam, digging small holes with her big toes. She looked. She hummed. She smiled. Being here was so much better than being home. She lived in Shawmut, Alabama, in the mill village where, if she had been home, she would have been in charge of her three little sisters, wiping noses, changing wet, dirty panties, feeding them, and trying to lead them in games like hop scotch. This visiting was far better than being home.

Engrossed in watching the crowd, she was not aware that there was anyone near her until she felt a hand clutch her right shoulder. Frightened, she turned and looked up in terror.

It was Mayhayley. She had apparently slipped out of her back door and trudged through the tall weeds, stepping over the rocks that had fallen off the old rock chimney that still stood majestically, yet barely attached to the house. Mayhayley often told Willis and a few others that she got tired of listening to that "stuff" so she slipped out and took a break every hour or so. She was making just such an escape when she happened up on Willis's cousin who she had seen on several afternoons lately when the cousin followed him down to her house and helped Willis bring in her wood.

"Don't be scared of me," Mayhayley said. "I know you're Willis's cousin. I've seen you at the Hemmings' house. Don't be scared of me," she pleaded, still holding onto the girl's shoulder. "I used to sit close by here on a stump myself when I was a little girl. I'd sit and think up things and sometimes I'd walk down to that old log house that's down there in the woods, where the Bassetts lived when they came here in the 1850s. The Bassetts were my forebears, if you know what that means. They died off or moved off before I was born, 'least I don't remember them. That old house most-near fell down last year, but it's still something to see," she said, as she pulled on the little girl's shoulder. "I got time."

The little girl hesitated until Mayhayley began to tug on her arm insistently. Mayhayley took a step toward the old house down in the woods, which they could faintly see. The girl followed Mayhayley and they slowly walked through the weeds, brush, and brambles. As the girl pushed the briars away, Mayhayley continued to talk about how it was when she was a little girl.

"Back then, there were flower beds and peach and apple trees along the road," she told her. "The trees dropped hicker' nuts, walnuts, and pecans way back then and there was a little stream down in the woods. It ran with cold, blue water that tasted so good. There must have been thirty little springs around here, just a-bubbling up clear water back then," Mayhayley said. "But no more, now that everything has grown up and the men-folks who cleaned out the springs are buried up on the hill at the Lancaster Cemetery or over at Caney Head. Now there is no one but me and Sallie and Sallie would rather play the piano than do any work," she whined as they walked toward the nearly collapsed, heavily leaning Bassett house.

When they arrived, Mayhayley shoved aside some kudzu vines that enveloped the building and gingerly stepped through an opening that had once held a door.

From inside, Mayhayley beckoned to the little girl to follow.

"No, ma'am," she mumbled. "I'm not gonna' go in that house."

Mayhayley scowled. "What? Are you afraid of me? I like children. I don't bring harm."

"Miss Mayhayley, I ain't scared of you. I'm scared of snakes."

"Afraid of snakes? Why are you afraid of snakes? Snakes won't harm you unless you hit at them. There have always been snakes here, maybe even when the Bassetts lived here. You know snakes live in most folk's rafters. Why, I bet there's snakes all in that Bledsoe house you're staying in, which I now own. There sure enough used to be under that house. I've seen them myself, rattlesnakes big as your arm. I use to crawl under that house when I was your age and see 'em all twisted up together. Snakes ain't nothing to be afraid of."

The little girl was not convinced, so while Mayhayley cajoled, the little girl's bare feet grew even more solid to the ground.

Mayhayley gave up and walked back to the door opening, and resting there with one arm holding on to a board, she looked directly into the eyes of the little girl and confidentially said, "Don't many people know it, but here's where I get my power. This, and the double veil. You ask Willis. I told him all about it."

"Told him what?" the girl asked.

"I told him that I come down here when I get wore out from the people who come to see me."

"What about the power you get here? What you telling about?" she asked.

"I'll tell you and when you get to be as old as me, you can tell everybody else what I said. When I was little like you I'd come here and those snakes you're afraid of would crawl all over me and I'd lie down on the floor in this room behind me. The snakes were long and fat and while I propped my head on that fireplace mantelpiece that fell down, they just crawled and squirmed all over me and I'd be just as contented. I guess we were friends because when they crawled between my legs it didn't upset me one bit."

Still standing in the doorway, Mayhayley continued, "Then I started bringing an old Bible down here and I'd read the Bible to them snakes. Sometimes I made up the hard words because I was just a little girl, but the snakes calmed down and they rested while I read to them. Then I got to tearing out the pages of the Bible and I'd lie here and chew on those pages after I crammed them in my mouth. The Bible says, 'You will eat the words of my mouth and you will be blessed, saith the Lord.' He was talking about prophecy, and that's what I do. That's my business and I learned how to do it right here. Right here," she repeated.

The little girl did not know the Bible. She only knew what her aunt read to her and Willis at night. She had never heard any of this.

"The Lord saith, 'Eat my words. They will be sweet in your mouth.' And they were sweet in my mouth and the Lord keeps on blessing me to help those in need. That's what I do," Mayhayley said with finality.

Then, she suddenly seemed to remember the crowd up at her house that did not know she was not there. "We'd better go back up to the house. Those poor people count on me to help them. I count on them to help me, too," she said, and she gave a little laugh. As they walked back toward the house through the bushes, Mayhayley added, "I saw the Devil in there one time, too. Next time we'll bring Willis down here with us and I'll tell you about him, too."

Mayhayley and the little girl hurriedly walked up the trail. When they got to the stump, the little girl sat back down again, but Mayhayley continued around to the back of the house and went inside.

The child sat for a while again watching the crowd, then she headed back to the Hemmings' house to tell Willis about her adventure with Mayhayley. As she walked, she thought about how frightened she should have been in that desolate, spooky place with Mayhayley, and how she was not. She had just been afraid of the snakes, not the snake charmer.

Afterwards when the two saw each other, Mayhayley would remind her, in a confidential voice, that she was ready to go back down to the old Bassett house and tell her some more about the Devil and what she promised him and what he promised her. But the girl-cousin went back to Shawmut before she and Willis and

Mayhayley could go back down there. The girl and her family later moved to another mill village up near Sylacauga, Alabama. She never came to Mayhayley's again.

As the years passed, Mayhayley and Willis came to trust one another explicitly and that trust evolved into a new "job" for Willis. Well before the Hemmings found Mayhayley, she had found the bug numbers game. "Playing the bug" was the biggest gambling game in Georgia during the twenties, thirties, and forties.

While Mayhayley dealt in playing cards, palm reading, horoscopes, and almanac predictions, and read configurations of the stars and moon, she was also busy selecting numbers that were "lucky." That was just what the bug number gamblers needed, lucky numbers, she explained to Willis.

One day when Willis came by to see if there were any chores, Mayhayley led him to the back stoop where another boy, Marvin Noles, was busy scribbling a series of three numbers on tiny slips of paper. Willis sat down to help; though at first he had no idea what they were doing. Marvin, who was immersed in the paperwork, promised Willis he would explain later.

Marvin finally got around to explaining the bug number phenomena: "Back in the twenties when playing the bug was really big in Georgia and around the country, one of the strangest things happened. A train wrecked outside of Atlanta and a picture of the train's damaged engine was in one of the Atlanta newspapers. The engine's numbers were very big and many bettors who saw the photograph turned in the engine's numbers as their bug numbers."

"That same week, the wrecked engine's numbers and the weekly bug numbers were the same!" Marvin said. "So many bettors used the engine's numbers for their bug numbers that the bug was bankrupt for a month or two until the pot could build back up. It was told around, that Mayhayley gave the engine's numbers on the train BEFORE it wrecked and she knew the winning bug numbers, too!"

According to Marvin, the story spread because so many people won and then the bug number seekers grew and grew until they were coming to Mayhayley's house from Roanoke, LaFayette, Anniston, Mobile, Atlanta and Chattanooga, and some said from as far away as Chicago!

Mayhayley paid Willis and Marvin a dime for their work, and some of the customers tipped them. Sometimes, Willis and Marvin led special customers to the back of the house so they could quickly see Mayhayley and escape the long Thursday and Friday lines.

Mayhayley was now asking her customers to split their winnings with her. Willis often delivered her money that winning bug number bettors felt compelled to pay her. The bug numbers racket was lucrative—that is, for the ones who were lucky, and an inordinate number of Mayhayley's customers were.

Willis found this side of Mayhayley curious. He knew that she was highly opposed to anyone drinking alcohol. She said that chewing, dipping, or smoking tobacco was bad and she urged her customers and her newspaper readers to stop the filthy habit. She believed divorces were harmful to children and should be made more difficult to obtain. She shamed fighters and was horrified at the killings around her, but for all her moralizing, she apparently was not opposed to gambling. Now that Willis thought about it, he should not have been surprised. After all, he had seen his family and their neighbors attend and participate in events where cakes, assorted prizes, and even farm equipment were raffled off. He had also seen some of the school boys play with dice.

In Willis's later life a cigar salesman swore to him that he delivered little King Raleigh cigars and he and Mayhayley and Sallie sat on the back steps and "lit up." Mayhayley did what she wanted, he learned. And while a few of their neighbors and most of the local preachers ranted and raved about card-playing, Mayhayley kept a pack of playing cards in full view and she used them to tell fortunes whenever she "damn well wanted to."

Once he became a part of the bug number business, Willis also began to notice the differences in Mayhayley's clientele. The well-dressed customers who came for their fortunes did not always recognize the tiny slips of paper that she handed them at the end of their visits. Those who appeared poorer (and were often black) and came to get their bug numbers were sometimes bewildered by her talk about, "a sweetheart with dark hair," or "you'll marry twice and have three children," or, perhaps, "you will have a bad car wreck." They only recalled the three numbers that Mayhayley gave them and for weeks and sometimes months, they bet those numbers over and over until they "hit" or didn't, and then they came back for some more numbers. Mayhayley attempted to please both types of customers and for awhile, the bug number seekers were the majority.

Willis also noticed that Mayhayley charged a higher fee for a bug number than her usual fortune-telling fee of $1.10 ("a dollar for me, and a dime for the dogs," she said.) Mayhayley's bug number business brought her large amounts of money and occupied her weekdays, while fortune telling was more popular on weekends. The bug number business also brought criticism from some of her white customers who did not like waiting for those "niggers" to get their bug numbers. When Willis told Mayhayley of the complaints, she said that they'd all stay in the same line and Mayhayley reminded him that their money was the same color as "they'rn." And that was the end of that, he said.

Too, some of the neighbors and family members who worked around Mayhayley's house selling soft drinks and candy bars became fearful that they might get in trouble with the law because of the bug number racket. Mayhayley assured them that there was nothing wrong with "giving out lucky numbers," and that's what she did, she insisted.

"One woman from Miami flew to Atlanta and took a taxi cab all the way down here just to get Mayhayley's bug numbers. Truth is, I was writing out the numbers at the time, so she really got mine," added Marvin. "Then, three or four weeks later this same woman came back driving a white, Coupe de Ville. She told Mayhayley that she had won 'big.' She offered Mayhayley another twenty dollars for her lucky bug number, but it was really one of mine," he said, then he laughed out loud.

When Willis was eighteen, he came to Mayhayley with a young woman on his arm. They told her they wanted to get married. Mayhayley gave them the money for their marriage license. Several years later Willis and his young family moved away to another farm.

When the John Wallace trial was held in Newnan, Georgia, in June 1948, Willis went to the Coweta County Courthouse, hoping to see Mayhayley. And there she was in all of her finery, a side of Mayhayley that Willis had never before seen, even though he had heard others speak of Mayhayley's early days when she wore crepe dresses decorated with ribbons.

During her testimony he heard her announce that she was "The Oracle of the Ages," something he had never heard before!

During a recess of the trial, they met in the upstairs hall. She was glad to see him and offered to tell Willis's fortune for free, just to recall old times. "Willis, we had a good time back then, didn't we?" she asked, as they stood among the crowd, many of them pushing and shoving others just to be near her.

"Yes, ma'am, we sure did," he replied. "Has that old Bassett log cabin fallen in yet? The one where you told us about the snakes and devils and things?" he asked.

"I don't recall telling you and that girl-cousin all those crazy things, now did I, Sallie?"

Sallie nodded. "Haley, you know you told those children all those things. I remember you did."

"Well, if I said it, Willis, it must have been so. Lawyers don't lie. It's against the law for lawyers to lie to little children."

Willis never saw Mayhayley again though he did attend her funeral. His wife was sick and couldn't go, but Willis went and sat through the service feeling sad that Mayhayley was gone.

He always believed that Mayhayley had turned his family's luck around.

They were indebted to her, starting with the squash seeds.

∾

WILLIS HEMMINGS was born August 2, 1919. As a child and young adult, he lived in Heard County and was a neighbor and fast friend of Mayhayley's. He worked for her often throughout his childhood and teen years performing various tasks ranging from laborious chores to helping choose lucky numbers for Mayhayley's fortune-seeking clients. He later lived in Coweta County and operated a fish and bait shop on Highway 34 outside Newnan, Georgia. He died December 18, 1998.

2

The Eyes of the Law

FOLKS COULD SEE J. C. OTWELL'S STATE TROOPER CAR COMING DOWN THE road long before it got there. He drove the four-door Ford with the red flasher faster than most because he could read those roads the way Mayhayley might read the palm of a hand. J.C. knew where to find the deep mud holes and the sharp granite slabs that would destroy the tires of vehicles driven by those less familiar with the unpaved roads of Heard County. Even at high speeds, his driving skills helped him avoid potholes and sharp rocks, the very same kind of rock that J. C. had heard put out Mayhayley Lancaster's eye.

The story that J. C. first heard was that Mayhayley was walking along the roadside, as was her usual manner, with all those dogs following, when a speeding car zoomed by, kicking a flinty rock into her eye. J.C. knew that tale could not have been true because Mayhayley had been without her left eye long before fast vehicles like that existed. One of her relatives later told J.C. that he believed she had been born with only one eye, further confounding the other strange birth stories that swirled around Mayhayley.

In the summer and the fall of the early forties, J.C.'s state trooper car stirred up billowing clouds of white and pink dust that lay thick and deep on the roads. The swirling dust kicked up by car tires was like a smoke signal to local residents. The farm families were either working outside in the fields or were in their houses with the windows open to the world. A cloud of dust was quickly spotted. It always held the promise of a much-appreciated visit or a message that something important was happening. Hard work could justifiably come to a temporary halt under those conditions. Of course, for the superstitious, the dust cloud often was a portent of bad news.

When a vehicle stopped, the women and children stood quietly and shyly at their posts, watching and waiting, while the men-folk staunchly stepped forward to greet friend, relative, stranger, or just J. C.

J. C. always brought smiles to their faces. He was jovial, with a big-toothed smile, and his tall, muscular frame looked good in his gray-green uniform. He carried a large, black pistol in a slick and shiny holster on his belt. He spoke with a loud, authoritative voice.

"Seen anybody who looked peculiar come this way?" he would ask.

"You haven't seen any speeders or drunk drivers coming through here lately, have you? If so, just let me know," he would remind them.

"These crazy folks who come through here looking for Mayhayley are driving like a bat outa hell," he might comment. Then he'd pause and ask, "They don't give you any problems, now, do they?"

If it was in the winter or early spring, when the clay roads were slick with mud and tires had wallowed out tracks nearly a half a foot deep, J. C. still drove faster than others. He knew if he got stuck, somebody would find a mule or a tractor and pull him out of the deep ruts. They were happy to oblige, they would tell him.

Then, J. C. would ask, "How much you charging for freeing those society folks on their way to Mayhayley's? Nothing? You don't charge even fifty cents for all that work? Man, you must be some kind of crazy!" Then he would laugh.

He might say, "Can you beat it! Here it is as cold as a tiches witty and there are five cars up at Mayhayley's! Where do you suppose those nuts get that kind of time and money to throw away?"

J. C. was quite familiar with Mayhayley. He often patrolled the area around Mayhayley's house and tried to help keep the traffic under control, especially on weekends when the out-of-towners would show up at her doorstep in droves. Through the years, he had grown fond of Mayhayley, in part because he had seen the good things that her work could do for people.

Once, during the summer of 1944, when the war was raging (J. C. had been deferred for a bad leg), he was stationed near Mayhayley's house. He had gotten out of the patrol car for some air. It was hot sitting inside on the slick hard seat, and he was leaning up against the car door trying to catch a breeze.

The crowd was big and growing. About eight cars were there and probably twenty-five adults were standing around or sitting on the front porch. Everyone was waiting patiently to see Mayhayley; besides that, most had no other place nearly as interesting to go. While they waited, they talked, told jokes, laughed, and proudly shared stories about Mayhayley—experiences that they'd had or heard about. J.C. knew they were believers or they would not have been there on a weekday. The tourists came on the weekends.

J. C. looked up to see a newer-looking car, one he had not seen before, with an Alabama tag. It slowly turned into the packed-down cotton field that was now serving as a parking lot across the road. When the car stopped, all four doors opened and the occupants began to get out. They were better dressed than the usual weekday customers. Outside the car they formed a neat little group around an older woman who was the obvious center of their attention. Two men moved to her sides and lifted her arms across their shoulders, then stretched their free arms behind her back. Without actually picking her up off the ground, they were carrying her toward Mayhayley's house.

J. C. moved toward the tightly bound group and inquired, "Is there any way I can help you?"

"No, sir. We're bringing Mama over here to Mayhayley's to see if we can get any help. You see, Mama's always relied on Mayhayley, and the worst thing has happened. She just got word that Hector is missing in action. Hector's her baby. She's just so torn up. We thought we might see if Mayhayley could tell her if he's going to be coming on home. He was in the invasion of Europe, you see."

J. C. politely listened as he walked along with the family to Mayhayley's front porch.

Everyone in the yard grew quiet as word spread about the missing soldier. J. C. motioned to the others to move out of their way and he walked along with them, sort of clicking his tongue, as if to say, "tish, tish" to a chicken or a dog that was under foot. A path was made for them as they walked, and then the mother was helped up the rickety steps. Someone opened the hall door and the family group moved inside.

They stayed with Mayhayley for a long time, more than the usual twenty minutes, while outside the customers watched the door and waited.

When the Alabama group came out of the house, Mayhayley was with them. The mother stood upright and Mayhayley walked along beside her and patted her on the shoulder. The male escorts were faintly smiling and they conveyed a different attitude than when they first came to Mayhayley's house. The talkative man who had told J. C. about the purpose of the visit turned to J. C. again and said, "Miss Mayhayley said it was going to be okay. Hector will call Mama up on the long distance in about three months, she thinks. You can imagine how we feel, now that Mama is so relieved."

J. C. watched Mayhayley as she walked with the group through the yard and across the little dirt road to their car. She was not her talkative self today, as in the presence of such deep sorrow and worry, she, too, wanted to show respect to the concerned family. As she stood still and watched, the passengers loaded up in the car and slowly drove out onto the dirt road, heading west toward Alabama.

That fall J. C. happened again to be parked down near Mayhayley's log cabin and saw the car from Alabama return. He watched as the same woman and probably an older son got out of the car and confidently walked into the milling crowd. They joined the end of the line and patiently took their places. The man announced to J. C. in a loud voice that they had heard from Hector, that he had been wounded and had been unconscious in a Welsh hospital since last June. He would be coming home soon and they were going to go see him in a Tuscaloosa hospital! They wanted Mayhayley to know.

J. C. thought to himself, "I'll bet she already knows."

That was not the only time that J. C. was impressed with the power of Mayhayley. He knew about the two women from LaGrange who came to visit Mayhayley that same summer of the War. They had not lost anything. They just had nothing else to do that day but ride around in the country, so one suggested to the other that they might want to ride the thirty miles up to Mayhayley's house. The other agreed. When they were ushered into the presence of Mayhayley, she abruptly asked, "Do you know a Mrs. Johnson?"

"Yes," one replied. "She's my neighbor."

"Well, when you get home today, you go over to see her and tell her that Edgar's okay and for her not to worry."

Edgar was the name of Mrs. Johnson's son who also had been in the European invasion that June. His mother had not heard from him and she had been worried sick about her son until her neighbors returned with Mayhayley's message. Mayhayley was right about Edgar, too.

J. C. also knew that Mayhayley could be helpful to the law. For example, there was that time when she helped locate Newnan Bailiff J. A. Beavers's lost cow. Beavers had gone to see Mayhayley when the cow vanished from his pasture. She sat him down and had him pick two cards from her deck of playing cards. She then told him, "Go to the third house on the river road." Bailiff Beavers told an Atlanta newspaper reporter that he found a man right where Mayhayley said and that he had immediately confessed to taking the cow and led Beavers right to the hiding place!

Not long after that, in 1948, J. C. was transferred to Coweta County, where he again saw Mayhayley's work. J. C. was directly involved in the John Wallace case, so much so that when Margaret Anne Barnes, a Newnan reporter, wrote a book called, *Murder in Coweta County*, J. C. was a prominent character in the book and later was portrayed in a film by the same title.

John Wallace, a Meriwether County farmer, had been accused of killing Wilson Turner, one of his former hired hands. There was little doubt that Wallace was guilty, but his reputation as a mean and slippery character had all the law enforcement people involved in the case scrambling to find ways to seal the case against him. Knowing that Wallace was a regular customer of Mayhayley's, and knowing that Mayhayley had served as an informant on other cases, the talk turned to enlisting her help.

It was late one evening when Solicitor General Luther Wyatt wanted immediate action. Because J. C. knew the way to Mayhayley's house, even on a dark, moonless night, he and Jim Hillin, another law enforcement officer, were drafted to go see her.

When they arrived at her house, it was way past midnight and both Mayhayley and Sallie were asleep despite the ruckus of the dogs. The dogs barked, howled, and raced around one another and around J. C. and Hillin. Hillin became frightened and said he would kill one of the goddamned dogs if his leg got bit. J. C. said he felt the same way but they needed Mayhayley's help and killing one of her dogs would not be the best way to get their foot in her door! Of that, he was sure.

So after a lot of blam, blam, blamming on her door, Mayhayley finally lit a kerosene lamp and appeared in its light at a small window. Her gaunt, long-nosed face with its reflecting glass eye, apparently hastily popped in place, spooked both J. C. and Hillin. When the door was unlatched, the two officers quietly and respectfully entered her sitting room.

When J. C. asked about a John Wallace visit, she raised not one finger, but two, letting them know. Wallace had been to see her twice in the last week.

That night in April 1948, Mayhayley's behavior was unlike any J. C. had witnessed before. She moaned, she rocked from side to side, she screeched out "Fire, fire, fire," she spit into her low-burning wood coals, and then she slept and dozed or went into a trance. When she was awake again, she mumbled about well water, then she talked about the Chattahoochee River, and, lastly, she said there were flies all over Turner's body.

Though some of Mayhayley's information was not correct, enough was that J. C. and the large coterie of law enforcement officers from throughout Georgia were able to locate the remains of Wilson Turner.

Two months later, J. C. watched when Mayhayley and her sister came to the trial in Newnan. She greeted him as the old friend he was. He watched her magnificent performance and chuckled at her antics. There was no question as to who won the debate between Mayhayley and Wallace's attorney, Henson, who mistook Mayhayley for a fool. According to Mayhayley, when she looked at him she saw an ass!

When the trial was over and J.C. began to move throughout his four-county circuit again, he was in the Heard County Courthouse one day visiting the office of the new sheriff, Ezra Gladney, who was less patient with Mayhayley than previous sheriffs who had known her all the way back to the turn of the century. The trial had made Mayhayley quite famous across the region, if not the country, and that had caused a real problem in Heard County. Mayhayley was being robbed again.

Her first reported robbery was in 1934 but the incidents had grown and were becoming more common and certainly more dangerous. Her neighbors did not feel as safe as they used to be and as J.C. represented a sense of security to them, they wanted more help from the law.

In the past, in Heard County, any violence, murders, shoot-outs, fighting, and even the arsenic poisoning that killed four people, were all caused by their own. It was brother against brother over supposed insults to mom or sister, or maybe cousins harboring hard feelings about property lines or disputed ownership of a piano. Perhaps a love affair that had gone sour was the cause.

Folks in these parts understood about quarrels and took pride in dealing with them themselves. When liquor drinking escalated confidence into exaggerated insults they believed that calling in the law was a sign of weakness. Why, any red-blooded, able-bodied, male head of the household could settle most disturbances! The sheriff, the deputies, J. C. and even Mayhayley encouraged them to "keep it amongst yourselves," and they usually did.

But Mayhayley's robberies were different. Everyone knew tales of her wealth being stuck between mattresses and hidden in the chickens' freshly made nests or in the corn cob-laden, long-deserted pig trough. Some neighbors had heard that she went out at night and dug small trenches in the hard packed dirt and dribbled loose coins and dollar bills into the ground! With her eyesight so poor, she was probably unable to find her money later, but none of her neighbors would have considered robbing her, a pitiful half-blind woman. Her sister was almost as old and considered feeble. Her mother, poor woman, was nearly eighty-five and sickly when the first robbery occurred. No one they knew would rob them, they thought. They were wrong.

They asked J. C. who would be low-down enough to take advantage of three old women? Could it be that more criminals were coming into the county? Was it not true that Pretty Boy Floyd from up in Chicago had been seen down at Rudy South's house at Red Oak? They had always heard that Jesse James and his brother, Frank, had hidden out down on the Redlands Road in an old log cabin owned by James's Roanoke, Alabama, cousins.

The frightening thing about these robbers was their audacity. During the incident in the thirties, the robbers had boldly gone into the Lancasters' house and rummaged through their things while the helpless trio watched. When Mayhayley's mother foolishly tried to intervene, one of the robbers grabbed her by the arm and tossed her fragile body into a wall. That was something no local criminal would do, they believed.

"J. C.," asked one coggitty old farmer, "what's the law going to do about Mayhayley's robberies? She was walking by here just yesterday with that damned pack of black dogs following her, when she upped and stopped and said she figured she'd been robbed thirty times during the last three years. She said they got at least $3,000. See how she's always dealing in them 'threes'?"

J. C. knew some of these tales were pure fiction so he just laughed and tried to calm their fears. The robbery when her mother had been attacked had been printed on the front page of the Franklin newspaper, so there was no reason for Mayhayley's exaggerations then. And J. C. knew that she really had been robbed at least twice, and these recent robberies had taken place when Mayhayley and Sallie were gone, staying with their sister, Mary, up at Stoney Point. Their fear of the robbers was now sending them packing at night, seeking refuge in the houses of anyone who would take them in. Because they could be unpleasant house guests, the hospitality of their friends, neighbors, and relatives was growing thinner. And thinner.

About a month before, when Mayhayley and Sallie returned home from an overnight stay with some relatives, they found the furniture shoved around the room and stacks of newspapers slung throughout the small house. The mattresses had been ripped open and the chickens, cats, and dogs were all over the house, muzzling through the mess. Mayhayley claimed she had been robbed of "$900.00 and some change." J. C. set up a meeting with Sheriff Gladney before the Heard County Grand Jury investigated both him and the sheriff!

Everyone knew that Mayhayley was vulnerable. Tales of her hidden wealth and of her staying away from her house at night made her place seem easy pickings. J. C., county deputies, and even the sheriff himself had begun to patrol the area more closely. Sometimes they parked their plainly marked cars on the dirt road that led to her house or up on the Ephesus Road, in full view. The robberies subsided, but it was still a problem to Sheriff Gladney.

Tales of the robberies, either real or imagined, were continuing, the sheriff reminded J. C. There was no doubt that within the two months since the Wallace trial ended, the crowds at Mayhayley's had doubled, tripled, or quadrupled. A steady stream of vehicles of all types was moving through the county to Mayhayley's house. They were coming into Heard County on every road: from Wedowee and Roanoke through Omaha; from Carrollton and Roopville down Highway 27; from LaGrange and Newnan via Franklin; from Heflin and Bowdon down Highway 100. At Mayhayley's house there were now car tags from Illinois, Florida, Mississippi, and as far away as New Mexico.

Sheriff Gladney knew the money was pouring in to Mayhayley yet the county's meager resources were being depleted by having to use deputies to direct traffic as well as to guard her house. The "dastardly robbers," as Mayhayley called them, would certainly be about again and Sheriff Gladney was determined to head off any new crimes.

"J. C., I got it figured out. I want you to get all the state troopers that are free to come into the county. I'll get all the sheriffs that will help, and we'll get the city police and, by God, we'll form a motorcade and go up to Mayhayley's, find all that money and bring it down here and put it in the bank! What do you think of that?" he asked.

J.C. thought Gladney's plan was crazy. The new sheriff would not have a chance in hell of getting Mayhayley's money. There was no telling how she would take such an encroachment.

She might pull out a pistol. Didn't she turn on Sheriff Virgil Bledsoe with a gun for auctioning off her pig? One swell lady from over in Chambers County (Mayhayley referred to people from Chambers as being from "shit pots") came to the Heard County Courthouse to swear out an arrest warrant when Mayhayley whipped out a pistol, waved it in her face, and told her to get out! All the lady had done, she said, was to remark that she had waited all day for a palm reading while Mayhayley sang, listened to Sallie play the piano, and talked to some Mr. Barker about buying a Coleman lantern from his Franklin furniture store. And once Mayhayley had rushed to her kitchen to get a pot of boiling water to pour on Deputy Henry Heard when he came for a piano payment. She proudly kept a long sword hanging on her wall for threatening customers she suspected were drunk.

"That woman ain't scared of nobody," J. C. declared.

Still, Gladney had made up his mind and was planning on going up there to get the money if he had to go by himself! J.C. laughed and then volunteered to help. J. C. knew Mayhayley and thought she might trust him more than the newly elected sheriff.

Early in the morning, on a hot day in July, a stream of cars left the Heard County courthouse with lights flashing, but no sirens wailing. They drove the six miles to her house with J. C. leading the motorcade.

When they got there, J. C. jumped out of his car and rushed ahead into Mayhayley's front room leaving the other officers sitting in their parked vehicles. He had asked the sheriff to give him a chance to talk Mayhayley into accepting Gladney's plan. If it could be done, he would be the one who could do it, he ardently believed.

"Miss Mayhayley," he timidly began. "I brought my Kodak up here. I've got plenty of film and I want to take you outside and take your picture."

"What's that you're saying, J. C.?"

"Well, it's like this. The new sheriff says he's going to have to take some of the deputy cars off the road and he says that he thinks you'll be a whole lot safer if there was no threat to you and Miss Sallie. We'd like to help you open up a mighty big bank account at the Franklin bank."

"I got a mighty big bank account at the Franklin bank. To tell it all, I got bank accounts at banks all the way over to Birmingham, Alabama. What the hell are you talking about, taking pictures and opening bank accounts?"

J. C. started over. He explained that there were several members of the law outside and he knew how she respected the law and always wanted to do her duty. They had come all this way just to work with her. She, being a lawyer, knew all about enforcement and, by God, they were there to take all her money to the bank. He had a camera and he was going to take pictures of her doing her duty!

Much to J.C.'s surprise, Mayhayley quickly gave in. Perhaps she consented because she knew and trusted J. C. or maybe she was in a good mood and thought that the publicity would not hurt. At any rate, to the astonishment of everyone involved, J. C. and Mayhayley confidently walked out into her yard, amidst all the law enforcement vehicles. The officers respectfully stood around her and listened while she welcomed them to her home and announced that she would be in charge of her money as it was collected.

All day long they searched. Mayhayley's sister and brother-in-law came down from Stoney Point to search the barn and chicken houses. Sallie donned a white apron and led the search in the house. Adult customers and their children who just happened to be there also looked wherever they were directed. The officers gently tipped over washtubs and rusted lard buckets and gouged into abandoned bales of cotton.

All the while, Mayhayley presided over the event either sitting in a straight-backed chair set up under a shade tree or leaning over a bed sheet stretched out on the ground. It was the responsibility of any person who found money to bring it to Mayhayley. She then loudly announced that the money was to be put on the bed sheet for her to examine to see if it were hers. It was always hers.

As promised, J.C. took pictures. Everyone there was in the pictures, but the pictures were mainly of Mayhayley and of her house on the day that the money went to the bank. Someone did use J.C.'s camera and took a picture of the two of them together standing outside her house.

Late in the afternoon, Mayhayley changed her clothes for another picture to be taken outside the bank when they arrived in Franklin. She also put on a black-brimmed hat and got a purse. Two station wagons and three automobiles were stuffed with old, rusty wash tubs, large lard buckets, and several tightly bound sheets, all filled with money.

The long motorcade left her house with Mayhayley riding beside J. C. in the front seat of his state trooper car. The patrol car's lights were flashing and their sirens were wailing when the vehicles pulled up to the front of the Bank of Heard County. The president, a large courtly gentleman, waited outside. He posed with the officers, Mayhayley, and her family in front of the bank, Franklin's most imposing commercial building.

When the picture-taking was over and the containers were being carried up the steps of the bank, the bank president apparently smelled or saw something distasteful. "Stop," he ordered. "You are not taking that stuff in my bank. I'll not have uncounted coins and bills dumped on me. Sheriff, you'll have to prepare these funds for deposit. I'll not have this chicken mess and dog mess brought into my bank," he adamantly declared.

Mort Lipford, owner of a dry goods store across the square from the bank, offered his store as the site for preparing the money for deposit. He enlisted volunteers to count Mayhayley's money and for more than three hours, they stacked and counted new bills and the out-sized old dollar bills which had not been printed since 1926. They also counted and rolled pennies, nickels, quarters, and half-dollar coins as well as irregular and foreign coins that were found among the cat, dog, cow, horse, pig, and chicken excrement.

When early evening came and the money was properly prepared for deposit, the bank president again greeted the group. Mayhayley posed again for a photographer from the *Atlanta Constitution*, which reported that Mayhayley had deposited more than $32,000 in the Bank of Heard County that day. The *LaGrange Daily News* reported $8,000—either way, a hefty amount of money.

When the money was safely in the bank, with J. C. escorting her, Mayhayley went over to Lipford's store and individually thanked those who helped in the counting. She awarded each of the tired, exhausted, dirty-handed workers a dime!

Two years later, in 1950, Mayhayley returned the favor to the local law when she helped them locate a landowner and farmer from outside Corinth, Georgia, who had vanished on December 18 while everyone was busy with a hog-killing at his house. They searched for him for a day or so, then his wife went to see Mayhayley for advice.

"You'll find him in a ten-acre field, near the middle. You'll see blackberry bushes nearby," Mayhayley told her.

Friends, relatives, and law enforcement officers searched every field within five miles of Corinth, yet there were no signs of the farmer. Many began to believe that Mayhayley's credibility was now shot, but the following February 9th, it was restored. A hunter, out looking for rabbits, saw his dog dart into some brambles and began to bark loudly. Instead of a nest of bunnies, the hunter discovered a body with a shotgun lying next to it. It was an apparent suicide who had tried to hide his own body, J. C. said, but in spite of the plan, Mayhayley had found him! His funeral was held in Hogansville on February 14, 1951.

J. C. believed that it was his job to keep up with everybody, so he listened carefully and read everything. He read one day in the *Newnan Times-Herald* of a Greenville, Georgia, psychologist's father, G.W. Skinner, who had gone to Mayhayley's when his pistol was missing. She told Mr. Skinner to go ask "the biggest man you know. He has your gun."

Returning to Greenville, Skinner decided "the biggest man" he knew lived nearby, so he went to Bud Murphy, the biggest man he could think of. The neighbor listened carefully to the missing gun story, walked into his house and returned with the gun. Mr. Murphy said he had found the gun in his yard, it must have fallen out of Skinner's car when he had visited earlier. He just picked it up, he said, and had been saving it for the rightful owner! After reading this, J. C. laughed out loud and said, "A-mazing!" but then J. C. was always amazed at Mayhayley.

Four years after the farmer's suicide, J.C. watched another parade, somewhat like the one he and Mayhayley led to the Bank of Heard County. This one carried Mayhayley to her last resting place at Caney Head Methodist Church. People came out of the woodwork for the funeral and controlling the traffic was a problem.

J.C. was there, not only as a law officer to help control the traffic that turned out for the funeral, but also as a mourner, a friend, and an admirer of Mayhayley. As he watched the hubbub, with his head filled with thoughts of the Mayhayley he had known, J. C. shook his head and smiled that big toothy grin.

J.C. OTWELL was born April 20, 1910. He lived in Newnan most of his life and was warden at Carroll County Prison and sergeant in the Georgia State Patrol for many years. He dealt with Mayhayley many times in his career as a law enforcement officer and was portrayed in the movie **Murder in Coweta County**. He died January 23, 1999.

Above, Mayhayley and J.C. Otwell. July 19, 1948. Below, interior of Mayhayley's house. Opposite page, top, Mayhaley, J.C. Otwell and two unidentified boys and a dog, helping count money; bottom, unidentified youth and Sallie.

3

A Critic's Eye

ETTIE JANE DUNAWAY SEWELL APPRECIATED THE GENIUS OF A GIFTED performer. She was one herself. In the early 1900s she had been the toast of the Chautauqua Circuit, a nationally popular lyceum and amusement enterprise. Through twenty-six years of helping her husband, Wayne, run their own production company and then Dunaway Gardens at Roscoe in Coweta County, her eye for acting talent had been honed to a fine focus. As she stood just inside the front door of the Garden's Blue Bonnet Tea Room, she found herself impressed by the talents of the curious woman who sat at a small folding table under the gazebo.

It was early spring of 1942 and the weather was still nippy. Hettie Jane wore a light sweater to ward off the chill, but the woman at the gazebo was wearing a heavy and ancient Army coat and hat. The coat was cinched around her frail body with an odd assortment of belts and colorful sashes. She was slightly hunched, as if fending off the cold while telling the fortunes of two young newlyweds. The couple had been married the day before under the "wedding oak" located just behind the Tea Room and was now staying a few days in Dunaway Gardens' honeymoon cottage, "Shangri-La."

Mayhayley and the couple were framed by a backdrop of rock streams and pools that tiered down to the gazebo area. Hettie Jane watched from a distance. She had known her share of fortune tellers. Growing up in Arkansas, she had seen the carnivals and traveling amusement shows that strayed through her hometown of

Conway. In her youth, Hettie Jane had been drawn to the sideshows, foregoing the delightful terror and excitement of the creaking Ferris wheels and wooden roller coasters, for the charms of bearded ladies and ten-cent-a-reading psychics.

Perhaps, she thought to herself as she watched the performance underway at the gazebo, those fortune tellers of Hettie Jane's youth had imprinted in her that initial desire to act. She had certainly recognized way back in her youth that they were actors, not clairvoyants. They simply spoke so vaguely and circuitously that no one could question the truth of their predictions, nor discern a concrete meaning. The result was that gullible, susceptible country rubes always heard what they wanted in the words. But not Hettie Jane. She had not a superstitious bone in her body and was not a woman to trust in dim predictions or fate, though the fortune she and Wayne now enjoyed was made in part on illusions.

Wayne and Hettie Jane had made a hefty living through their touring company, which traveled from one small, southern town to another producing follies and plays with a handful of itinerant young actresses and raw local talent and egos. Wayne had started in the business in the early 1900s, working initially out of Atlanta, for the Affiliated Lyceum Bureau of America.

He circulated from town to town with a script, a "professional" actor or two, and all the costumes and sets for the play. In each town, he enlisted the support and sponsorship of a local church, charity, or civic group to produce the play, splitting the proceeds with these deserving causes and filling the roles with locals eager to show off their natural born theatrical gifts, real or imagined.

That's how Hettie Jane had met Wayne, back in 1913, when her own career was flying high. Hettie Jane had gone to college, majoring in elocution and other spoken arts, and had become a star of the Chautauqua circuit. She had toured the United States extensively and established a reputation for her exquisite monologues. In fact, she was one of the highest paid dramatists on the circuit, making about $300 per reading. Hettie Jane had come home on a short sabbatical from touring and had grown bored with the tedious day-to-day life in Conway. She decided to attend a ladies club meeting with her mother and sister just to break the monotony.

It was there that she first laid eyes on Wayne. He was in town promoting a show and was the speaker at the meeting. She would later learn that this was the key to making the shows work. He would visit with different groups in the town before the show opened and, like a revival preacher, he would talk up the production passionately. He was so accomplished at it that he often worked the entire community into a frenzy to see the mayor or preacher or some well-known socialite often acting the fool in the plays. Local curiosity and vanity, not fine theater, drew the crowds.

Immediately, Hettie Jane was taken with Wayne. "His cameo face, his glorious hair," she had written of him to a friend. He took to her as well. Back then, her hair was swept up like a Gibson Girl's and her buxom figure turned many a man's head. They courted for three years, still pursuing their separate careers. They had been so busy, marriage was not initially discussed, but their bond was sealed when Wayne took ill on a trip to Arkansas and Hettie Jane nursed him back to health. She remembered how he had seemed so fragile and so thankful for her succor. She fell completely in love with this more tender, needier side of his charismatic self.

They married in 1916 and Hettie Jane moved with him to Atlanta, then to Roscoe, just outside of Newnan, ever near Atlanta, where they started their own touring enterprise. The plays, performed through the Sewell Production Company, were shoestring productions with sentimental themes and scripts. Hettie Jane wrote most of the plays and the scripts were far from intellectual. *Here Comes Arabella*, *Miss Blue Bonnet*, *Black-Eyed Susan*, and *Tantalizing Tillie* were among their biggest hits, though they certainly did not rival Shakespeare.

One of their production chiefs, Sarah Cannon (better known as "Minnie Pearl," a name she adopted while working with the Sewell productions) said, "They were the worst plays you could ever imagine." Putting on theatrical productions in ten-day's time, which was typically all the time they had in each town, required plots and dialogue that were easily learned and simply produced, according to Minnie Pearl. Since it was the only entertainment that many townspeople could find, lack of sophistication was not an issue.

The shows made the Sewells and the specified charities nice sums of money, even through the Depression. Wayne became famous for his entertainment empire, acquiring the nickname, "Ziegfield of the South." Hettie Jane knew that one reason they managed to thrive during the Depression was Wayne's belief in diversification. He had his finger in many financial pies, including farming. He was among the first farmers in their area to grow Austrian peas, which proved to be a valuable crop for many small farmers in the South.

Wayne was fearless in his ventures. She still smiled to think about the dancing bear that Wayne had bought for a song from some sideshow. He thought it could be the beginning of his own carnival. He kept the unhappy creature in their giant, old hay barn, but even when it was quiet, it caused a commotion. No one could ride past the place on a horse without it bolting when it caught a whiff of the bear inside. Neighbors finally told Wayne he would have to get rid of the bear, which he did. Hettie Jane was never sure what the bear's final fate was; some things Wayne kept to himself.

A whiff of the food cooking behind her in the Tea Room's kitchen brought her back to the present. She had hired a professional chef who specialized in a mixture of Southern and French cuisine. The odd assortment of tastes had been a smart move and the Tea Room had become a novel place for locals to eat, as well as popular with many famous and semi-famous visitors to Dunaway Gardens. Mayhayley daintily ate in the Tea Room when she had a break.

Hettie Jane was proud of the Gardens, and rightfully so! The enterprise was drawing such notable entertainment personalities as Walt Disney, dancer Edwin Strawbridge, and actress Tallulah Bankhead who came through the gates to enjoy the company, the countryside, and the labyrinth of rock gardens and woods within the twenty-two acres. It had been Hettie Jane's idea to turn Wayne's old family plantation into a retreat for actors and a training center for young women whom she and Wayne hired to manage and perform in Sewell Production Company's shows.

The site took up only a tenth of the plantation. It sported numerous buildings, including the Patch Work Barn where they practiced plays and trained the girls in the summer, before sending them on the road. In addition to the Blue Bonnet Tea

Room, there was an amphitheater, housing for the young actresses, and cabins for visitors. "Shangri-La," the honeymoon cottage, was the fanciest cabin where they usually housed their more famous visitors.

Hettie Jane was proudest of the rock formations and gardens dotting the property. They were built of fieldstones that grew better than any other crop in the soils of west Georgia and east Alabama. The granite stones were placed in whimsical arrangements according to Hettie Jane's vision and diligence, not by chance. Hettie Jane had not physically placed them herself, but she had designed and engineered their construction. She hired local workers at fifty cents a day to follow her directions. She also paid ten cents for each fieldstone, which were brought by the wagon loads from a several-county area. That seeming pittance was a godsend for many who were struggling in the tough times. Hettie Jane thought of herself as a private version of the CCC or WPA — giving people jobs and a purpose in the midst of a national financial crisis.

Hettie Jane was totally dedicated to Dunaway Gardens and she usually kept a close eye on the daily schedule. As she stood watching the mismatched trio, she should have been in the kitchen directing the chef, but she could not tear herself away from the scene at the gazebo. She stepped outside the screen door and took a seat on the steps of the Tea Room to watch more closely.

The first time she heard the name of this fortune teller — Amanda Mayhayley Lancaster — was in the late 1920s. It came up shortly after John Simms, one of the Sewell's tenants in Roscoe, had skipped town on a three hundred-dollar bond Wayne had signed. Desperate to retrieve Simms and regain his money, Wayne tried every normal way possible to track down the man, to no avail. Marjorie Dunaway, Hettie Jane's niece, who had come to Georgia to learn the acting trade and had become a road manager for the company, half-jokingly proposed that Wayne should, "Go ask Mayhayley." Wayne had laughed out loud.

Like many people with roots around Heard County, Wayne knew of Mayhayley. He had told Hettie Jane, when they first married, about Mayhayley and how she had been plying her trade there for as long as Wayne could remember. He also told her that many people swore by her accurate and helpful predictions, though at the time he had never visited her himself. In fact, his only personal encounter with Mayhayley had been on an Atlanta street sometime around 1913.

Wayne had described the scene to Hettie Jane. He was striding along the sidewalk when he spotted a bizarre-looking woman walking toward him. She wore garish colors and a dress shorter than most women dared to wear at the time, for it actually showed her knees above her high-topped Victorian shoes. Her tall figure was crowned with a big hat that seemed as if it could fly right off her head, with all the feathers that dangled from its brim. His first thought was that she must be some sort of actress, but as she drew closer to him he saw she was wearing a patch on one eye, and looked more like a man than a woman. Wayne could not fathom why an actress would wear an eye patch just to attract attention, though he had heard of weirder things. In later years, he would have known the term "cross-dresser" and would have called her that!

As the odd figure grew closer to Wayne, she gave him a withering stare with her good eye. He sensed that there was about to be trouble of some sort for just then, he heard loud laughter coming from another man close by. To Wayne's good fortune, another man had seen her and dissolved into raucous laughter at the sight of the strange-looking woman. He was laughing so hard he had to lean against the brick side of a store building and hold his sides. Mayhayley abruptly stopped, turned away from Wayne, whirled around, and marched up to loud-laughing man and asked in a very loud voice, "What's so goddamned funny?"

Wayne slipped away before she took further notice of him as well, but he left wondering who that woman could be. Soon afterwards he heard of a woman, looking somewhat like the lady he had seen on the street, who had confronted prominent lawyer Sid Holderness in the Carroll County courtroom. It seemed the woman had interrupted a court case with a distracting, noisy entrance. She was wearing a heavy, woolen army coat with epaulettes and two rows of bright, brass buttons down the jacket front and on its cuffs. Her matching woolen skirt dragged the floor behind her with a flounce of red cords hastily sewn in a haphazard, curling design. To top it all off, she, too, wore a black, tight-fitting hat with a red, feather boa draped around her head, which flopped over her army coat and danced toward the floor.

Mr. Holderness had stopped his summary presentation to stare. Being a fun-loving, self-confident guy even in the august halls of the court, he shouted, "Well, here comes Christmas!" All, including those already looking at her after hearing the loud slam of the heavy wooden door, turned to look and, as the man on Peachtree Street had done, burst into loud guffaws.

Not to be outdone, the woman glanced around the room and, after an ominous silence, shouted back at them all in her own loud voice, "And there'll be no Christmas presents for you!" Mr. Holderness slumped into his seat. The spectators told this funny story over and over and, when Wayne heard it, he was convinced that this must be the same woman he had seen that day on the Atlanta street. Both were Mayhayley! When Wayne heard that Mayhayley claimed to be a lawyer, he was intrigued and wondered to himself if she were a lawyer-playing-actress or an actress-playing-lawyer?

Despite his admiration for Mayhayley's theatrical flair, Wayne was hesitant to go see her about the Simms matter. It had been many years ago since he saw her on that Atlanta street, but he somehow feared she might recognize him and identify him with that laughing crowd. So, he called Marjorie's bluff by asking her to go for him.

As Hettie Jane recalled, Mayhayley gave an audience to Marjorie, handing her a deck of cards to hold as soon as the young woman took a seat. Marjorie had not yet told Mayhayley the reason for her visit when Mayhayley said: "You want to know about John Simms?"

Marjorie had gasped aloud, but Mayhayley ignored her obvious shock and continued: "He left at night in a truck or car, I don't know which, and crossed the river at Carrollton. He spent two days in Anniston, and then went on to Birmingham. He's staying there now with a family and is working on a road crew. You will find the home of these relatives near a filling station and a store on the edge of town. I see him brought back here in three days."

Marjorie had hurried home to Wayne, who in turn sent one of his workers to fetch Simms. Sure enough, Simms was at a relative's home, which was located near a filling station on the edge of town. Simms later mentioned that he had, indeed, spent two days in Anniston on his way to Birmingham.

The remarkable outcome piqued Wayne's curiosity about Mayhayley and a few months later, Wayne went to see her himself. On that visit, when she didn't seem to recall their first encounter many years before, Mayhayley told him four things: he would go on an unexpected trip, his car would overturn, he would be robbed, and he would become ill. In a matter of a few days, all four prophecies came true. Wayne told these experiences to reporter Susan Messer who quoted him in an August 1930 *Atlanta Journal* magazine's full-page article about Mayhayley.

Mayhayley's name came up again when Tallulah Bankhead was in the area visiting a friend in Carrollton. Tallulah had just returned from England where she had spent ten years performing on the stage. Her shows in England had been successful and she had gained a reputation for being a daring performer. Executives in the booming American film industry and on Broadway recognized that her sex appeal could make them money and had lured her back to the United States.

It was not uncommon to see Tallulah in the South for she was a native of Alabama. She often visited her father in their Jasper, Alabama, home when he was home, relaxing from his duties as an Alabama congressman. She also went to Montgomery to visit her aunt and uncle who were making a name for themselves as Alabama's eminent historians. Between family visits, she sometimes called on a childhood friend who was now living in Carrollton.

Tallulah's friend, Lucile Long Stewart, had married well and was living in a large, Georgian-style house. Hettie Jane and Wayne often visited Carrollton, too, and knew the opulent house and it owners well. The house was a not a landmark because of its ostentatious presence but because right beside the house was a miniature replica of the big house: a doll house that was the envy of all little girls who visited or lived in Carrollton.

Lucile was thrilled at the chance to entertain Tallulah and had dropped hints about her impending visitor for weeks — telling the butcher, the florist, and everyone that she had an important guest coming to her house. She invited the Sewells to a party for the actress, telling Hettie Jane that Tallulah would appreciate having some of her "own kind" around for the evening. Hettie Jane was not sure if that comment was meant as a compliment or an insult, but she and Wayne accepted the invitation, regardless. It never hurt to spend time with celebrities.

The guests were already there when Tallulah arrived to the customary hugging and kissing and cheerleader-type squealing, typical of some female reunions. The elegant actress grabbed a drink and immediately began to rant about the loss of a diamond ring, one "nearly as big as the Hope diamond," she said. Hettie Jane suspected that this was an exaggeration, but tried not to let her doubts show. She was accustomed to dramatic people, being one herself, who stretched the truth. She was also quite capable of putting on a poker face. Tallulah moaned that she could not possibly continue her trip to New York and see that special sweetie who had given her the ring, since it was gone and she had lost it.

Hettie Jane recalled the entire evening in detail. Tomato juice was served to the Baptists and mint juleps were passed out to the Methodists, Presbyterians, and Episcopalians, while Tallulah insisted on champagne. The guests were served dinner outside on the terrace and the Stewart children were willing to help out in order to see their mother's grand friend who wore slacks, talked with a hoarse voice, and smoked cigarettes. Those cigarettes dangled constantly from Tallulah's painted fingernails and punctuated her comments throughout the evening. The topics included: Tallulah's lost ring, the benefactor who gave it to her, the London stage, the royalty who adored her, the lost ring, upcoming opportunities on the New York stage and films, and the lost ring!

Later that evening, after Tallulah had retired to her quarters, Mr. Stewart escorted Hettie Jane and Wayne to the door. He had obviously gotten his fill of Tallulah. He whispered to them that he had a solution to the lost ring. "I'm going to send Lucile and Tallulah off to see Mayhayley Lancaster tomorrow. She'll shut up Tallulah's missing ring monologue," he had said conspiratorially.

After a luncheon at a neighbor's house the next day, the two old friends took off in the Stewart's black car with directions from half of Carrollton. They got lost three times on the twenty-five mile journey, but were always able to get new directions. Finally, they found the unpaved lane, the cotton field parking lot, and the log cabin. They also found a yard and porch full of other adults waiting to see Mayhayley.

They bided their time, sitting in the car recounting tales of high school fun and describing boring homework from unbearable teachers. About the time their reminiscing ran dry, they realized that they were the only customers left in the yard, so they quickly got out of their car and rushed toward the front porch where a lone figure stood, leaning on a four-by-four roof support post which was slightly bowed. They later learned it was Mayhayley's sister, Sallie, who ushered them into the dark room where Mayhayley sat.

Tallulah took a seat on an old piano stool near Mayhayley and, in her well-modulated voice, told Mayhayley about the lost ring.

Mayhayley quietly listened, then leaned toward Tallulah and intensely peered into her face, so it was told that evening at a large party hosted by the Stewarts' friends.

"Tallulah became quiet." Lucile's husband had to stifle a laugh when this detail was mentioned.

Mayhayley continued to sit and stare at her. Finally, she said, "Shadow!"

"Shadow? What do you mean 'shadow'?" Tallulah asked her.

According to the story, Mayhayley did not answer her question, but after a brief interlude, said, "The ring is in a quilt. I see the ring amongst a quilt that has red and yellow and blue and green and white squares. Go home and look in the quilt and you'll find it. That's all I know. If you'll go in three days, you'll find it. If you wait longer, you may not. Go find the quilt."

That was all. No more conversation. Tallulah got up from the stool and paid Sallie some money. The two women rushed out of the house into the yard and into the quickly arriving dusk. Soon they were riding like bats out of hell to make it home in time for another party in Carrollton.

That night, at the party, Tallulah swished up to Lucile and announced that she would be leaving in the morning to return to her family home in Jasper, Shadow Land.

"Shadow Land!" Lucile exclaimed. "Of course. That's what Mayhayley was talking about when she kept saying, 'shadow, shadow.' She was telling you the name of the house where the ring is."

Early the next morning Tallulah's bags were loaded in the car and she returned to Jasper.

Hettie Jane and Wayne later learned the outcome of the trip home. When Tallulah got to Jasper she went into "Shadow Land" and wandered from room to room looking for the special quilt that Mayhayley had described. First she searched the quilt on her own bed in her childhood room. No ring in a quilt. She moved through the house into her sister's bedroom, her father's bedroom, and a guest bedroom. There was no ring in any of the neatly folded quilts that were lying on the beds.

Then she climbed the steps to the attic which she had plundered a few days earlier in search of some old costumes. When Tallulah opened the attic door, she saw an opened trunk that she had pilfered on the previous visit. Resting on the inside shelf of the trunk was a quilt. It was red and yellow and blue and green and white. She bent over and picked up the quilt and gently shook out the folds.

Clink.

Oddly, just a few days after Hettie Jane heard the story of the found ring, Mayhayley had shown up at their Tea Room. It was not uncommon for Mayhayley to take her fortunetelling on the road, setting up a stand in a friend's parlor or even at nearby courthouses. When she was last in Newnan, she asked if she might set up a table at Dunaway Gardens. The sight of Mayhayley had made Hettie Jane almost recoil — she was haggard and her face was heavily lined and leathery. But Hettie Jane was no fool. Mayhayley could be quite an asset to the Gardens, as a form of entertainment. So, for the past week, Mayhayley had been plying her trade under the gazebo. People came to get a reading and the Tea Room was doing a booming business, even though this was not the busy season for the Gardens. Hettie Jane credited Mayhayley for the increased activity.

The couple rose from their seats under the gazebo and headed toward the Tea Room. Hettie Jane rose from her seat on the step to greet them.

"How bright is your future?" asked Hettie Jane as they came close to her.

The couple, linked arm in arm as though they could never be pried apart, were glowing. "She said we'll have a son who'll grow up to be a teacher," they stated in unison. Then they swayed past Hettie Jane and into the restaurant to toast their future.

Psychic or not, that Mayhayley was one hell of an actress, Hettie Jane thought to herself. Someday, Hettie Jane might ask her to travel with one of her drama groups.

Hettie Jane never got around to asking her and Mayhayley had other fish to fry, anyway. In June 1948, Mayhayley became embroiled in a murder case twelve miles away in Newnan. While it was often said that Mayhayley was "discovered" in the Wallace trial, the Sewells and others had recognized long ago that she was a star. It was the Wallace case, however, that resulted in more newspaper articles about Mayhayley, as well as the October 1948 nationally distributed *Front-Page Detective* magazine story that featured her!

Oddly enough, Wayne's name was drawn for the John Wallace jury box, or venires, as some called it. He was not selected for the jury box as was G.Y. Chesnut, C.W. Hardy, C.E. Whitlock, Willie Plant, Joe Will Dukes, R.L. Bowers, J.J. Farmer, Jr, A.B. Carmichael, C.E. Newby, W.C. Neely, O.W. Prince, and Homer Lassiter. They, like he, were prominent, white males who, in some instances, were personal friends of the sheriff, Lamar Potts. His not being chosen often caused him to wonder if it was a coincidence that he was not needed on the jury or was it some of Mayhayley's doings?

Hettie Jane and Wayne kept up with Mayhayley by reading news stories and listening to their friends talk about trips to Mayhayley's cabin. Dunaway Gardens began to sink into obscurity and the road signs that touted the beautiful gardens became rusted, rotten, and worn. Mayhayley's fame continued to grow and soon the

Sewells heard that she had built a big, new brick house and the barbecue that announced its opening had attracted more visitors than had ever been at Dunaway Gardens on a single day!

Hettie Jane and Wayne lived on in Roscoe until moving into Newnan where niece Marjorie, a popular schoolteacher, was living. Hardly anyone mentioned the glory days of Dunaway Gardens except a handful of the Sewell's closest friends and the occasional interested preservationists from the Georgia Trust.

When the Sewells heard of Mayhayley's death in 1955, they decided to attend the funeral. It was held on one of the most beautiful spring afternoons they could remember. Marjorie drove them to the Caney Head Methodist Church where they joined the large crowd jockeying for seats inside the small sanctuary. They found seats and waited for Mayhayley's last grand entrance.

Religious music was played loudly on an upright piano. Mounds of fresh flowers were massed against the stage. The audience was just as they liked it: rich and poor, strong and crippled, fancy-dressed and ragged, the brazen young and the sniffing old, along with young families holding crying babies. It was a magnificent production!

"What an act," Wayne murmured to Hettie Jane as the service started.

When they heard of the epitaph Mayhayley had carefully chosen for her exit, Hettie Jane was again in awe of Mayhayley's theatrical flair. The epitaph read:

Neither did his Brethren believe in Him.
Saint John, Seventh Chapter, Fifth Verse

While some dolts thought that it was blasphemous for Mayhayley to compare herself with disbelief in Jesus's power, the Sewells disagreed.

"What a line!" they both said.

HETTIE JANE DUNAWAY SEWELL and her husband, WAYNE P. SEWELL were well known entertainment industry figures in the Southeast during the early 1900s. Both were involved in the theater business and they encountered Mayhayley at various times in their careers, coming to admire her gift for drama as well as fortune telling. Hettie Jane, a native of Arkansas, was born on August 20, 1870, and died December 12, 1961. Wayne, a native of Roscoe, Georgia, was born June 7, 1877, and died April 13, 1965.

Left, the photograph of Mayhayley that appeared in Front-Page Detective *magazine, October, 1948. The picture was made by Atlanta Consititution photographer Ryan Sanders for a 10-page news story titled "Prophet of Doom."*

Below, Mayhayley poses with Celestine Sibley and other reporters from Atlanta Constitution, Summer, 1948.

4

Eyes in Crawfishes' Tails

JOHN WALLACE SAT WITH HIS BROAD BACK AGAINST THE COLD CONCRETE wall of his cell, the weight of his heavy state-issued boots pulling his feet awkwardly toward the floor from the edge of his cot. He ran a hand across the short stubble on his closely cropped, partially bald head. His polar-blue eyes stared at the wall across the room.

Wallace had just eaten his last meal. He had chosen the same plain, everyday prison fare that the other inmates had eaten that night. His arrangements for his own funeral had been made including the purchase of blue silk pajamas in which he wished to be buried. Some of his family members were waiting nearby and even some of his old Young Harris classmates had come to be with him. He had spent the last two days writing letters to his compatriots.

Despite all the execution-related attention, he still did not feel afraid, because he did not believe he was really going to die in the next few hours. It could not happen. It had not happened on his previous three times when he faced the electric chair. Sure, he had run out of appeals, but he knew it would not happen because Mayhayley Lancaster long ago told him that he would live to be an OLD man. It was 1950; he was only fifty-four; he had many years yet to live, or so he ardently hoped.

Wallace believed in Mayhayley deeply, despite his fury over her testimony against him in court. During the two years since the trial, through all the appeals, he had gotten over his anger toward her. He had "found religion" and had decided that Mayhayley was just like him. He felt their lives, and fates, were linked.

Wallace's relationship with Mayhayley had begun in the 1920s when he was a young man, before he had become one of the most feared and powerful men in his county. He traveled the thirty-five miles or more from his home in Meriwether County to Mayhayley's place in Heard County many times through the years seeking her advice. The first time he went to her was when a bin of hand tools had disappeared from his tool shed. She told him that he had just forgotten where he put them and they were probably at the Strickland place. He found the tools in his granddaddy's cow barn stuffed in his own leather bag.

The next time he went to see Mayhayley was when he lost a prized shotgun. Sure, he had a lot of other shotguns, but this particular one had belonged to his Uncle Mozart Strickland, Wallace's idol. Mozart had raised him from age eight following the death of Wallace's daddy in Chambers County, Alabama. His uncle had seen that Wallace got a good education, sending him off to Gordon Military School at Barnesville, Georgia, and to Young Harris College in north Georgia.

Mayhayley told him that one of his hired hands had stolen the shotgun and he would probably get scared and bring it back in three days or three weeks. Wallace did not wait for the gun to come back; rather, he went on a rampage of the houses on his 2,000-acre dairy farm. When he found the shotgun, at the second house he entered, he grabbed a shovel and brutally beat the young white man nearly to death. Wallace told Coweta County Sheriff Lamar Potts of the beating while languishing in jail after his trial for the murder of Wilson Turner, a farmhand on the Wallace place. To Wallace, beating farm hands was acceptable. It was the best way to teach them to keep their hands off his things. He did not really mean to hurt him badly, he told the sheriff.

Wallace would never have told Mayhayley about the beating because he knew that she abhorred violence. Strangely, Mayhayley did not object to people who flaunted the law by making or running whiskey, playing craps, poker or other card games, or playing the bug numbers; however, Wallace knew that tales of fighting or alcohol consumption often resulted in Mayhayley banishing even her most loyal customers from her house. She refused to see ruffians. Wallace did not want that to happen to him, so he kept his mouth shut about some of his more violent deeds.

John Wallace went to Mayhayley every six months for years, looking for lost or stolen items such as a prized dog, some money, a ring, a fine saddle, and an old Bible he used in his Sunday School class at his local Baptist church. He told her about the loss of some milk cans from his LaGrange dairy business. He told Mayhayley about some whiskey missing from one of his many liquor stills. Once, he told her that a complete liquor still had disappeared from his woods. During the years, Mayhayley advised him about his personal life, told him he would marry, and even predicted how long he would live. In every instance of missing property, she gave him either vague or specific instructions where to look and her advice about his personal affairs had always been useful and amazingly accurate, too. She was correct so often, it kept him coming back and forth to her house over the years. He was a firm believer.

Wallace was not ashamed of his belief in Mayhayley, either. He had spent many a sweltering, summer night with other men on the square in Greenville beneath the clock of its stately courthouse trading gossip and lies. On those nights, he often bragged about his belief in Mayhayley, who was well known to folks throughout Georgia, and beyond. Hell, one night he even told the group that he and Franklin Roosevelt shared a common belief in fortune tellers.

"When he was governor of New York, Roosevelt got off the train up in Atlanta to go see a fortune teller named Alice Denton Jennings," claimed Wallace one night. "She told him, right there in front of the group going with him to Warm Springs, 'In your palm, I see power.' With that horse-faced, no-nonsense wife of his looking on, she also told him, 'You're going to be the president of the United States.'" Wallace and other people in Meriwether County took great stock in what Franklin Roosevelt said and did. To them, he was a citizen of Meriwether County, living so much of the time in nearby Warm Springs. Wallace often took pride in saying that he went to Mayhayley Lancaster and Roosevelt went to "that woman up in Atlanta."

Wallace's real trouble had started with a visit to Mayhayley in mid-April of 1948. Wallace had gone to see Mayhayley about some missing cows. She told him that "Turner" had taken the cows, which infuriated Wallace. John Wallace was not a man to be tampered with so he set out to retrieve his cows and avenge the affront that Wilson Turner had made on his pride and against his authority.

Two weeks later, John Wallace was back to see Mayhayley about Turner's missing body. He was searching for the remains of Wilson Turner, whom he had murdered and thrown into an abandoned well somewhere in the wilds of his huge estate. Having forgotten the location of the well, Wallace was panicked that the law might find the body before he could. He needed to find it so he could fully dispose of the evidence. He believed that without a body, a murder conviction could not be forthcoming. That was the law, corpus delicti, in Georgia, he reminded her. She reminded him that she knew the law better than he did, she being a lawyer and all.

Mayhayley had helped him both times. It was not until much later, when he sat in the Coweta County Courthouse and listened to her testify against him, that Wallace regretted his visits to Mayhayley. While Mayhayley's reputation as an informant was well known to law enforcement persons, such as Solicitor General Luther Wyatt, John Wallace only then learned of her double role.

Wyatt had grown up in Centralhatchee, a small community in Heard County not more than six miles from Mayhayley's house. He was aware of her stock-in-trade fortune telling and had even visited her once himself. On his wedding day, Wyatt had taken his new bride to see Mayhayley, just for the fun of it. Now, he was a prominent Troup County attorney who had recently been elected Solicitor General of the four-county district. He would be prosecuting Wallace for the murder of Wilson Turner. Their case was less than airtight. In fact, they needed that body badly.

Witnesses had seen Wallace beat Turner, seemingly to death, at a restaurant just inside the Coweta County line, but before anyone could stop them or call the law, Wallace and his men had sped away taking Turner with them. Apparently they had hidden the body well, leaving no solid evidence that a murder had taken place. Still, Wyatt and Sheriff Potts were sure that Wilson Turner was dead and that Wallace was the culprit. They were desperate to find some leads and to prove their case.

Since his election, Wyatt had learned through the law-enforcement grapevine that Mayhayley was a very useful informant. People told Mayhayley things they might not tell anyone else and often turned to her in times of fear, hoping to make sure they would not be caught. For years, lawmen from as far away as Ruston, Louisiana, had relied upon Mayhayley for information that she garnered from unsuspecting customers.

Luther Wyatt enjoyed telling one story of how a routine trip to Mayhayley's by local officers helped nab a LaGrange man who had robbed the post office. Apparently, the man who committed the robbery had gone to Mayhayley to ask if he would be caught for his deed. The customer naively told her all about the robbery—how he and several others broke into the central post office at LaGrange and stole bonds, which they had hidden under a manhole downtown among the main water pipes in the sewers. When he asked Mayhayley if he would be caught, she answered, "Most probably," knowing full well that she, herself, would certainly turn him in.

"Are the bonds still there?" she asked him.

"Yes, ma'am," he replied.

When officers came by for their bi-weekly fact-finding visit, she told them the whole story. The officers went right back to LaGrange, crawled under the street, and found the bonds. The robber was arrested for the crime and tried in a public courtroom, where Mayhayley came to observe the trial. He was found guilty and sent to the federal penitentiary, apparently never realizing that Mayhayley was his downfall. Mayhayley justified her informing on her customers by telling that it was her duty as a citizen to contribute to a law-abiding society. At John Wallace's trial she said over and over, "I'm just a doin' my duty."

When Wyatt found himself in the dark about the alleged John Wallace crime, he thought of Mayhayley. He sent two deputies up to see her and she told them enough to get them on the right track to the body, or what was left of it. Her words "Fire, fire, fire," caused them to look for signs of a recent fire on Wallace's plantation. Her information gave the investigators some directions and soon after Otwell's and Hillin's visit to her, the law enforcement officials found what was left of Turner, whose body had been retrieved from the well by Wallace and two reluctant, terrified black farm hands. Turner's body had been burned to ashes that were dumped into a stream in Wallace's woods. The fire's massive explosion had burned surrounding trees, and the scorched leaves led the investigators to the site.

On a Friday, one of the hottest days of June 1948, Mayhayley and Sallie were driven toward Newnan in a state-trooper car. On the twenty-five-mile trip, they stopped in Franklin and Mayhayley went alone into the Lipford store where she fingered some merchandise, purchased nothing, and remarked as she went back toward the state car, "I guess you know I'm all tied up in that John Wallace mess. I wish I weren't." The owner of the store later said she appeared to be very proud of the notoriety she was getting.

Newnan, the county seat of Coweta County, was a small Georgia town known for its beautiful homes and a semi-industrial status and railroads, attributes that Heard County's county seat was missing. When Mayhayley and Sallie arrived, they were escorted directly to Sheriff Potts's office, across the street from the massive, red brick courthouse. Potts's staff, the attorneys for both sides, and other members of the courthouse staff met them at the sheriff's office. Some of the courthouse workers were also present just because they wanted to see Mayhayley.

She had never appeared before at the Coweta County Courthouse in this capacity. Only older persons remembered her from the 1920s and 1930s when she came to the courthouse to bid on property at the sheriff's tax sales. Back then, she was always dressed in a finery of silks and satins, feather boas around her neck, shiny brooches pinned on her clothes, dangling earrings dripping from her lobes, and rings and bracelets all over her hands and wrists. Most of the people standing outside the courthouse on that swelteringly hot, humid day only knew Mayhayley from her more recent days of rags and that Army hat. Her imagery had grown to include twenty or more black, scrawny dogs, skinny mules and cows, rotting bales of cotton, and the old log cabin deep down in the woods of Heard County.

She appeared like a vision from her long ago past. She stepped from the patrol car wearing a satin, shiny red dress festooned with snorting yellow dragons. Her dress partially covered her high-topped, black shoes that had small heels that lifted her to a height equal to most of the men standing around her. On her head she wore a bright red Shriner's fez. It gave her trouble all day slipping around her head, even though there was a five-inch hat pin with a large red stone on the end. (The same hat pin appears in early portraits of Mayhayley.) The pin was also much like the one that rumor said had put out Mayhayley's left eye years before.

This day, Sallie, her sister and seemingly constant companion, wore a floor-length black dress and a black Jackie Kennedy-type mourning veil that completely hid her face and reached to her shoes.

After the preliminary meeting in the sheriff's office, the two over-seventy women moved into the crowd that had congregated in the yard of the courthouse. They headed for the door to enter the building and its courtroom. A path was opened for them. Some of the people spoke to Mayhayley, asking for predictions about the trial; some pressed dollar bills wrapped around dimes into her hand. When one spectator told her that he had bet money on Wallace being found innocent, Mayhayley quickly retorted, "Well, a fool's pay is a fool's way."

She continued her trek around the courthouse grounds taking money and dropping it either into her bosom or into the small stringed purse she was carrying. She bantered with the crowd where one newspaper reporter heard her remark, "A dollar and a dime—will buy the Spirit's time!" She was smiling with a nearly toothless grin and holding Sallie's arm as they walked up the steps between the massive two-story, Doric columns that grandly framed the entry to the marble-floored, cavernous corridor inside.

As Wallace sat in his cell, two years after the trial, he recalled how surprised he had been to see Mayhayley at the trial. He had seen Mayhayley's entrance as he, too, walked toward the courthouse door from the jail, his home for the last month and a half. He was casually strolling, arm-in-arm with his very pretty wife and her father, a seven-term Florida judge. Wallace waved to his friends, smiled at strangers, and exuded an air of positive confidence in the outcome of his case. After all, he had always gotten out of tight spots in the past. When he saw Mayhayley standing in a knot of followers in the upstairs corridor of the courthouse, he smiled again, thinking that she was there to support him.

Three days later, on Monday morning, when Mayhayley took the witness stand, Wallace realized she was not exactly on his side. On that day, Mayhayley wore the same clothes as the Friday before but a different hat. She assumed a somber, serious demeanor. When she was led into the courtroom to take the witness chair, all her smiles were gone.

After her swearing in, she took her seat on the stand and looked directly into Wallace's face. He had expected to see a glimmer of collusion in her face. There was none. He felt disconcerted by her detached attitude, but decided she was just assuming a "professional" demeanor in the formal courtroom setting. After all, she claimed to be a lawyer and Wallace knew she took legal issues seriously. He leaned back in his chair, arms crossed at his chest, and assumed a nonchalant and confi-dent— almost bored— pose that he maintained throughout the trial.

Her testimony began with questions from Luther Wyatt, the prosecutor. "Do you know the defendant on trial, John Wallace?"

"Yes, sir," she replied.

Wallace felt relief. She would surely defend his character.

As Mayhayley answered the next few questions from Wyatt, questions that established the fact that Wallace had visited Mayhayley twice after the murder, Wallace began to realize she was there to do him in.

"Did you ever hear him, on any occasion that he was there at your house, threaten to kill anybody?" Wyatt asked.

"Yes, sir," Mayhayley replied.

"Who did he threaten to kill?"

"A man I didn't know, said 'Turner.'"

Wallace sat bolt upright in his chair for a moment, then realizing that his action would be noticed by others in the jury and in the press, and might be taken as a lack of confidence on his part, Wallace forced himself to settle back into a relaxed posture.

Mayhayley carefully recalled the events of their visits, including the fact that she had seen a vision of a well. "I . . . told him there was some nails and green flies there, and they were taking the body out and putting it on a horse's back off of the farm where it was at, and muddied it somewhat so it would not be identified or finger prints found on the horse." At that, Wyatt closed his questioning.

A.L. Henson, Wallace's newly hired lawyer from Atlanta, began a cross-examination of Mayhayley's testimony and immediately began to question Mayhayley's "gifts."

"Now you are what folks call a fortune teller?" Henson asked.

Mayhayley protested that title, saying, "I am really called The Oracle of the Age."

"A what?" Henson retorted sarcastically.

"We were born that way. We are not made, like school teachers," Mayhayley replied.

The cross-examination fell into a sparring match between Henson and Mayhayley that focused mainly on her prophetic powers. When Henson tried to make her explain how she "knew things," Mayhayley replied, "The wise forseeth and hideth himself."

"You are just the wise forseeth, and hideth the information. Is that what an Oracle of the Age does?"

"I do many things. I buy oxen and mules," Mayhayley replied. It was obvious she was not happy with Henson's attitude, and she certainly was not going to give details about her powers to him.

Henson persisted. At one point, he asked her if she had seen the green flies with her natural eyes ". . . the ones you are looking at me with?"

"I have an artificial left eye," she replied.

Mayhayley eventually conceded that her visions came from the stars. Further pushing on Henson's part about how she could actually "see" things, resulted in Mayhayley's answer: "Crawfishes' eyes are in their tails, and mine is in my head."

The examination continued, with Henson trying to discredit Mayhayley's gift and Mayhayley leading and never giving him the satisfaction of a real answer. It was like watching someone taunt a cat with a string — Mayhayley would always yank it away just when Henson thought he could pounce successfully.

By the time the cross-examination was over, Wallace realized that, despite the silliness of her exchange with Henson, she might be his real downfall in the Turner murder trial. In all those years he had visited her, he had never known, that she was an informant. When Mayhayley left the stand, Wallace was livid that this gnarled old woman might have sealed his fate.

Anger toward Mayhayley lingered in Wallace for at least a year after his conviction. He often thought he would get even with her when he got out, which he had no doubt would happen. No one could keep John Wallace down for long, he ardently believed.

Now that four appeals had been denied by the state courts and the United States Supreme Court, Wallace was feeling less optimistic about gaining his freedom. Two and a half years spent behind bars also had given him a new sense of patience and forgiveness that he had never known before. Looking back on the trial, Wallace could almost chuckle out loud at Mayhayley's part in his downfall. When he heard that his lawyer Henson had said, "Not since the Seventeenth Century has the testimony of a witch been allowed in a court of law," he was able to laugh.

He admired her nerve and cunning. Those were traits he recognized in her the first time they met. She was like him, always able to talk her way out of a tight. They both were willing to go to the edge of reason for something they might want.

Sitting in the State Prison at Milledgeville, awaiting execution, Wallace thought about events a few months earlier when he was still in the Atlanta Tower, the holding site for those waiting to be moved to Milledgeville. Celestine Sibley, a reporter from the *Atlanta Constitution*, who covered his trial, came to visit him.

He gave her quite a show, affably directing the prisoners' activities in his bullpen and optimistically predicting that he would not be electrocuted. He told her how he had gotten religion in jail and had found a scripture promising that prayer would spare him. Besides, he told Miss Sibley, he had Miss Mayhayley's word that he would live to be eighty-eight years old! "If there was ever a time when I hoped she was telling the truth, this is it!" he said.

He thought those same words again to himself as he sat on the cot. He rubbed his hand over the stubble on his head, one more time, and said out loud to the four blank walls, "Whatever happens, Miss Mayhayley, I figure we will meet again sometime. In Heaven or Hell."

John Wallace was electrocuted Friday, November 3, 1950.

Mayhayley heard that Wallace's funeral was going to be over in Pine Mountain, formerly called Chipley, in Harris County at his wife's Methodist Church on the following day, a Saturday.

She said, "Well, he'll surely not come to my funeral."

Then, after a long pause, she declared, "And I'll be damned if I'll go to his!"

JOHN WALLACE was a powerfully influential farmer and businessman in Meriwether County who started visiting Mayhayley for fortune telling advice when he was a young man. Many years later, he was accused and later convicted of murdering one of his farm hands, and he consulted with Mayhayley during this time. She later testified against him during his nationally-publicized trial. He was born June 12, 1896, and died in the Georgia electric chair on November 3, 1950.

5

The Preacher's Wife Sees it All

CLARA BRYAN WAS IN HER FRONT ROOM PRACTICING THE PIANO FOR THE Baptist Church Sunday School Assembly. While she never professed to be an accomplished pianist, she could play as well as Jimmie Mae, Myrtie, Pallie, Elma, Maude (her Heard sisters), who all played, some by ear and some by note. As she worked on "Farther along, we'll know all about it . . ." her daddy's favorite song, she was thinking about how it was not easy being a preacher's wife. Lovic was not a preacher when she married him. If he had been, she doubted she would have been interested in the youngest of the Bryan boys who lived down the road from her. He had been called to preach after years of farming and working in a cotton mill where they and their children had lived in the mill village. Their lives were far better, now.

Being a preacher was not a full-time job, but with the four churches that Lovic held down, he was able to be pickier about the jobs he took. Together, they were able to run the farm they now owned, outright, and she got to spend her days any way she wanted. This morning she planned to practice the piano, put out some flower seeds and cuttings in her front yard, and, if the weather held up, get out the tractor and re-plow the garden. Maybe next week she'd plant her vegetables.

Clara's life was good and she was contented. Her only complaint was that she was expected to be nice to everybody (whether she liked them or not), to visit the sick of the neighborhood as well as at his churches, and do whatever else her husband asked her to help out in his ministry. She attended all the funerals and she did what she could to help with the dead and their families, including taking up money for funeral expenses. She knew her neighbor Mayhayley Lancaster was sick again and falling asleep a lot, but she had plenty of money to take care of everything and never would be a financial burden to anyone in the community.

As she sat half-playing and half-thinking, Clara heard a car door slam, and then another, ending her reverie.

She stood, closed the piano lid over the keys, and walked toward the front door, the door no family member ever used. She was certain these were visitors since she was not expecting anyone.

She peeped through the small, rectangular glass pane in the front door and saw a four-door yellow taxi cab. "Uncle Albert," she murmured. "He'll have either his wife or he's taken Tommie out of school again to ride around with him," she grumbled to herself.

As she opened the door, she saw it was her mother's brother, as she suspected, and, yes, he had taken his little girl, Tommie, out of school to keep him company. He had a small fleet of taxicabs, parked on Bull Street in LaGrange. He sometimes drove a cab himself and often came up to Heard County and rode around to visit family members. Most of them had left Heard County seeking work, but he enjoyed seeing anyone he could find at home.

As usual, he came in talking. He quickly said that he had a day with nothing to do so he'd taken Tommie out of school to ride with him. He also wanted to ride by Mayhayley's and settle her hash. He had about enough of her, anyway, the way she meddled in everybody's business and he was still mad at some of the things she had the guts to say to just anybody! He went on to tell his niece that one of the men who drove for him had ridden up to see her last week and had taken his wife along. "Would you believe, Mayhayley started in telling him that he had better straighten up and that he would benefit himself if he would quit messing around with his neighbor-lady! She said all of this with his wife standing right there!" Albert exclaimed.

When Albert stopped to catch a breath, Clara asked, "Well, Uncle Albert, was that man running around with his neighbor?"

"Well, to tell it all, he was, but don't you think that was some kind of bad meddling for her to start up a row like that?" he asked. Then, continuing, Albert began to tell why he was really going to see that troublemaker, Mayhayley Lancaster.

"What happened that brought me and Tommie up here was not so much what she told that driver last week, she does that sort of thing all of the time, but now she's gone too far with me! You see, last week my Bertha came up here and, she won't say why, but I think she was trying to find out where I was. As God is my witness, I don't run around like that, now do I, Tommie?

"As I was saying, my wife came up here to see Mayhayley about something and when she got to her cabin, Mayhayley wasn't there. My wife looked around and saw her down in the pasture trying to break up some dirt to plant some corn, so she started walking down to the field. As soon as she got to Mayhayley, she mentioned that, coming down through the pasture, she'd walked around a bloated cow with its stomach all stuck out and its feet straight up in the air.

"Mayhayley listened to Bertha real hard. Then she asked, 'You saw my cow all bloated up? My cow wasn't dead when I came down here to work. Her stomach damn sure wasn't all stuck out and its feet were not stuck up in the air, unless, unless' and then she said, 'you killed my cow!'

"Well, of course my wife denied it and said she never killed anything in her life—she didn't even kill chickens—she gets them dressed at the grocery store down in LaGrange. Then they sort of faced off to one another.

"Mayhayley started yelling at Bertha, 'You killed my cow, and, by God, you'll pay for it.' She yelled at Bertha and Bertha just stood there and took it, not knowing what to do. Finally she turned around and rushed back up the hill to Mayhayley's house where the taxi was waiting. She said she only turned around once, but when she did, she heard Mayhayley yelling and cursing her real bad and saw her shaking her fist at her, too. When she got home she was still so upset, she couldn't eat any supper. She says she doesn't know what Mayhayley is saying about her, maybe telling everybody that she killed her cow, and God knows what else! So, it's Bertha that wanted me to come up here today and straighten her out. And that's what I intended to do when I came up here this morning but, then the dad-gumdest, funniest thing just happened.

"When we go up there, I marched right into the house because I'm one of the few people I know who's not scared of her. But when me and Tommie walked right into her room, there was Mayhayley standing in the middle of that messed-up place just a laughing and talking to a crowd of those Paschals from up at Carrollton. When she saw me—I'll never know if she knew why I was up there or not—she turned towards me and began to tell them all how I was a Cosper. And then she said she'd taught all the Cospers and their relatives, the Sheets and the Souths over at Red Oak School and what fine folks we all were. She reminded her sister, Nancy Paschal, who was standing right by her, that their oldest sister, Sarah, had married Jim Cosper, one of my older brothers, and how they all now lived in Walker County, Alabama. She said, again, what fine folks we all were are—all us Cospers. 'Aren't we all family?' she turned and asked me.

"Then, without stopping for breath, Mayhayley began to call out to Sallie to come out of the kitchen and play the piano for everybody. She reminded us that Sallie was a great piano player and had taught piano in Texas and in Carrollton, too. 'One of the best piano players I've ever heard,' she told us.

"I don't have to tell you, Clara, none of us believed that, but we just stood and didn't argue. Even I've got enough sense not to argue with Mayhayley about Sallie!

"When Sallie rushed into the room, she went over to Mayhayley and got that piano stool that Mayhayley was using for customers to sit on. Sallie shoved the stool over to that old, dusty, upright piano. Then she swept a lot of papers and books off the keyboard onto the floor and sat down.

"Before Sallie touched the keys, though, she got up and peered down into the piano. Mayhayley explained to us that Sallie was looking for her music books, as she was a trained musician who did not play by ear, like most everybody else did. She said Sallie could read those piano notes. I guess Sallie didn't see any books in the piano, nor anything else as it turned out, so she wheeled up the stool and sat down on it again.

"We were all standing real quiet with Mayhayley all rared back in her rocking chair. She was looking so proud-like as Sallie spread out her fingers on both hands and began to bang on those keys, I mean all over those keys. She ran her fingers up and down that keyboard and she was stomping on the foot pedals. She began to sing some old church song like 'Jericho Road,' when I saw a big, fat, black cat peep out of the top of the piano. While I was looking and Sallie was doing what she was doing, that cat jumped out of that piano and landed on the floor right in front of Mayhayley's chair, but ran off before Mayhayley ever saw it. Then another cat, a kinda yellow-looking one, looked out over the top of the piano and it jumped. Then another.

"About that time I saw some little kittens start coming out from underneath the bottom of the piano. One baby kitten climbed up on Sallie's foot and Sallie was giving that kitten a ride to beat the band! Cats were spewing out of the piano like it was a volcano. They were meowing and screeching, yet Sallie kept on playing and Mayhayley kept on smiling and rocking. When one of the big cats jumped from the piano on to Mayhayley's lap and knocked the playing cards all over the floor, Mayhayley came to her senses. She looked around the room and shouted, 'Sallie, stop all that goddamned noise and get back to your work!'

"Clara, we were so astonished at all that but we were too scared to laugh out loud, so we all just stood and stared while those cats and the kittens scurried off and crouched in the corners of that crazy room.

"It was over. Tommie and me walked over to Mayhayley and she patted Tommie on the head. She didn't say anything else and I didn't either so we came on out and got in the car and came on over here. Have you ever heard of such a thing as that? Have you ever heard of a concert like that one?"

Clara was laughing with Albert and Tommie. She was thinking how her day was turning out far better than she expected when she had heard the car doors slam. She joined in with her own Mayhayley story, as she pulled little Tommie up into her lap.

"I'd known Mayhayley all my life, but right after Lovic and the children and I moved up here by the old Bryan homeplace, I got to see a new side of her. We weren't more than a mile from her house and we'd just gotten settled in when a big rainstorm came up. We gathered the children in the house and sat still. With all of that lightning and thunder and those big, strong summer raindrops beginning to hammer our tin roof, we knew that we were in for a typical Heard County summer thunderstorm. All of sudden, without any warning, our front door swung open and in busted Mayhayley. She was drenched. Her clothes stuck to her and water was running off her head and down her arms and legs. She wasn't cursing. She wasn't even talking out loud. In fact, I'd say she was sorta whining and I'd even say she was keening. That woman was scared to death.

"Lovic went over to her and led her to a chair and she sat there and took deep breaths. Then, Mayhayley stood up and dragged that very chair you're sitting in over to a corner. She turned the chair towards the wall, looking all together like a child who'd been sent to the corner for misbehaving. We sat still and just watched and listened while she made some strange moaning sounds," continued Clara.

"In a little while, the lightning and thunder moved on and the heavy rain slowed down and I got up and began mopping up some of the water that had come in when Mayhayley opened the door and dripped all over my floor. Mayhayley was still sitting in the corner.

"Pretty soon, after the rain was all gone, she got up and started talking and telling us how she hoped she hadn't interfered with us but the Thaxtons weren't at home and neither were Bud and Dessie, so she had just kept on coming and she was sure glad our door wasn't bolted up. Then she pulled her wet self together and out our door she went!

"That was the day I saw another side of Mayhayley. The neighbors later assured me that every time a storm came up, she was getting out of her house and going somewhere! See, little Tommie, some grown-ups are scared of storms, just like most little children. But I never would have expected to see Mayhayley so terrified of a summer storm as she was. I always felt a little sorry for her after that and I tried to treat her more kindly, since I knew that she was such a scaredy-cat!

"But, I still didn't want her coming to our house to get to be a habit, so Lovic and I talked about how we could get her not to do it again. The way we cured her of coming to our house in the thunderstorms, and we had them a lot and the rain would tear up our garden and beat down our plants, was Lovic went down there and told her I was bad off scared of lightning and thunder. He told her that I was just as scared as I could be, which was a big story, but by then he and Mayhayley had become pretty good friends and she believed everything he said. She told him that she understood that some people were scared of storms, but that she wasn't, which was a bigger lie. Still she never came back to our house during storms again. After that experience with her, whenever a storm came up, I'd stand at the door and watch her as she darted from house to house looking for a place to stay until it was over.

"Now isn't that weird?" Clara concluded as she put Tommie back on the floor, got up, and walked to the front door where she stood and looked out. Uncle Albert and Tommie joined her at the door and then they all walked on out to the taxicab, not saying anything else about Mayhayley.

During the forties, Clara and Lovic lived on in their house. That was when the bug number crowd was really coming and going up and down the unpaved road. Clara watched the cars, both swell ones and beat-up vehicles and after the John Wallace trial in 1948, strangers often stopped at their door looking for Mayhayley's house, but over the years Clara kept as much distance from Mayhayley as she could.

In May of 1955 when everybody was talking about how sick Mayhayley was getting, Clara was not surprised that Lovic suggested she go up to her new house and check on her. He did not think Mayhayley was going to make it much longer, based on what he had heard happened up there.

It seemed that Mayhayley had seen her last customer on Friday, May the 20th. No one could remember whose fortune Mayhayley had told that afternoon, but soon after the disremembed customer left, Mayhayley complained to Johnnie, Sallie's son, who was living with them that she "didn't feel so good." Johnnie yelled to Evie, his wife, to come fast. With Sallie looking on, Johnnie and Evie pulled Mayhayley out of her new overstuffed chair and stretched her out on her bed.

"Mayhayley lay still all during the early evening. Sallie went in and out of their bedroom checking on her and talking to her," Lovic had heard and, in turn, told Clara. "When it got late, bedtime, Sallie crawled in the bed beside Mayhayley and they both slept through the night."

The next morning, a Saturday, which would have usually been a busy day for Mayhayley, Johnnie shooed everybody off, explaining that Mayhayley was not well, but assured them she would be up and about soon. He urged them to come back. Really, Mayhayley was barely conscious. About noon Johnnie sent word to Lovic that they needed some help up there. When Clara got to Mayhayley's, she was mumbling and talking incoherently about something. Clara wished she knew what she was saying.

Everybody in the neighborhood knew this was serious. While Mayhayley had been sick a lot lately and had gotten well, Lovic was sure she was not going to make it this time.

Early Sunday morning, when everybody in the house was up and dressed, Clara came up to stay again and Lovic went on to Macedonia to preach. By the time Clara got to Mayhayley's, she had stopped turning and tossing in her bed and had become real quiet and still. Clara heard no more mumbling. "But, Mayhayley's quietness seemed to stir up Sallie's rising voice," Clara recalled.

They all watched Sallie moaning, groaning, clutching her stomach and wiping tears from her swollen eyes. She was walking the floor and resting only when she sat on the bed and called out to Mayhayley, begging her to wake up, to sit up, to get well. Sallie's calling didn't do any good.

By ten o'clock Sunday morning, Clara said she saw that Mayhayley's breathing had become labored. Sometimes, she opened her eyes. Her gaze darted around the room, not focusing at all. She would raise first one hand and then the other, fluttering her fingers up in the air. Clara recalled seeing dark frowns pass over her face. Mayhayley squinted her eyes. She seemed to be in pain, but she never asked for any help, not even water, which Clara thought was very brave of her.

When Mayhayley looked as if she was really hurting, Clara watched Sallie climb into the bed with her. Sallie lifted up Mayhayley's head and put her arm underneath her. With her other free hand, Sallie patted Mayhayley and talked to her. Sallie was now curled up around Mayhayley and was holding her tight, like she was her small child. Clara and the others in the room continued to sit and watch.

Mayhayley's youngest sister, Mary, from Stoney Point, had come and had taken over amidst the turmoil and was now stiffly sitting in Mayhayley's overstuffed chair. The men in the family stood quietly outside the bedroom or in the yard. They, too, believed that Mayhayley's end was growing nearer and nearer. Finally, everybody in the house was real quiet, including Sallie.

Clara watched as Mayhayley took in a deep breath. Then she breathed in another, even deeper breath, and made a choking sound. "The room was electrified," she later said. Then, as they watched, Mayhayley breathed in one last time, but never appeared to exhale. Everybody in the room stood up and, as if in a trance, moved around her bed. Mayhayley's face took on a pinkish glow as the last of her blood surged through her face. Her eyes widened in a frozen stare.

Sallie, who was in the bed with her, started screaming, "Hayley! Hayley! Hayley!" Then she grabbed up Mayhayley and began to rock her back and forth, both arms tightly holding her.

Somebody, Clara could not recall just who, went over and loosened Sallie's fingers from around Mayhayley's back. Somebody else pried Sallie's body off of Mayhayley's. It took several people to pull Sallie to the edge of the bed, to stand her up on the floor, and push her toward the door, then out into the front room. All the while, Sallie was still calling Mayhayley's name. Clara said she didn't get involved in that, she just sat still and watched like a good preacher's wife was expected to do.

Sister Mary left the room to call the doctor and the funeral home. Then, Clara also left the room, stepped out on the front porch, and wondered why Lovic had not come. She later remembered that, after all those hours in that dark house, she was surprised to find that it was a beautiful, bright May day and there were little breezes blowing over the yard. The land around Mayhayley's house was already plowed and ready for planting. The spring rains had come and gone and the trees, shrubbery, and wild flowers were putting out buds and leaves. As Mayhayley loved flowers, she had already gotten some flower seeds and annuals planted in the lard buckets strewed around her two front doors and in her front, side, and back yards. The new house amongst the flowers was a pretty sight to Clara, after the goings-on inside.

In the afternoon, a radio station in Carrollton announced that Mayhayley had died. Then, everything began to happen all at once. Lovic was there, and a man always knows how to take charge better than women do in a crisis, or so Clara thought. Other radio stations, in Newnan, LaGrange, and West Point, joined the Carrollton station with funeral details. The stations announced that the funeral would be Tuesday afternoon, May 24th, at the Caney Head Methodist Church at 3 p.m. and Lovic would be the preacher.

Dr. Doyle Caswell met the body at the funeral home that Sunday afternoon and signed the death certificate, listing heart failure as the cause of death. Unfortunately, there was no autopsy, which would have cleared up the ongoing rumor of her brain being sold prior to her death. Also there would have been less of a possibility of someone stealing her body from her grave to capture her head in the coming years, had there been an autopsy, some believed.

Soon, the neighbors were bringing in great mounds of food to feed the large Lancaster family. There were whole hams, platters of fried chicken, tin pans filled with baked chicken and cornbread dressing, glass bowls filled with potato salad, plates of deviled eggs, and sandwiches. Clara took pineapple sandwiches, she recalled.

In no time at all, the dirt road that led to Mayhayley's house was filled with vehicles. Some were brightly painted new cars; others were rusted-out older cars covered with dust and grime. There were also mud-caked pickup trucks, loaded down with children riding in the back. In some of the fancy cars, there were elected officials or county employees out from Franklin, or well-off customers of Mayhayley's who counted on her to "tell them what they needed to know." One group of visitors, to whom the family paid special attention, were the former students who said they remembered Miss Mayhayley from her early days as their schoolteacher. Some of the visitors claimed to be former business acquaintances of Mayhayley's from when she was a cotton farmer or when she owned the movie house in Franklin or when she had been the self-proclaimed "biggest mule trader in west Georgia." One visitor said he knew her as a saleswoman of flower and vegetable seeds. Clara believed that nobody else had ever known as many folks as Mayhayley did. Hundreds wanted to share in her last days on this Earth. Dead though she was, she could still draw a crowd.

The neighbors, family, and customer-friends mainly stood around and talked to one another on that Sunday afternoon. There was no carrying on, as there would have been had Mayhayley been alive and well. The sounds were of quiet voices, well-behaved, whispering children, the rumble of vehicles coming and going, and the sounds of car doors opening and closing. The dogs and cats were quiet and lay still, bunched up among each other.

One thing that kept everything quiet was the fact that Mayhayley's death brought together the dueling sides of the family. They were just barely able to be cordial after the recent dispute over Mayhayley's sanity and control of her money. Luckily, the duplex layout of Mayhayley's new house allowed the two sides to have separate quarters. Mary divided the donated food between the two kitchens but there was little communication between them. Mary and "her side" stayed in the right portion of the duplex where Mayhayley and Sallie had lived, while Johnnie and "his side" stayed in their usual quarters.

On Tuesday morning, the day of the funeral, a small group that had stayed outside the house all night long knocked on one of the doors saying they wanted to get in the house early, to avoid the long line. They were rudely refused entrance. One neighbor admitted that he had gotten in the funeral line "about three times" since he would not be seeing her anymore. He also recalled that he heard the remark, "Doesn't she look natural?" when, in fact, he didn't think Mayhayley looked natural at all! He said he had never seen her without her Army hat, which meant he had only entered her acquaintance later in her life. The neighbor told everyone that he had seen her every day and she looked so much nicer than before.

When lunchtime came, all the doors to the house were closed and locked. The family got dressed in their funeral clothes and posed for photographs in front of the opened casket. Lovic led a small prayer service when the other two preachers got there, for now Mary had invited Herman Caldwell, another Baptist preacher-friend, and the Reverend Sam Odom, the supply minister for Caney Head Methodist Church, to share in the funeral service. Before the casket lid was closed for the last time at home, Sallie, neatly dressed in a suit-type dress with matching hat, posed once again with her son Johnnie in front of the open casket. She, like Mayhayley, wore a corsage on her left shoulder.

Right at two o' clock, Sheriff Virgil Bledsoe, who was now the sheriff of Heard County after seceding his father Charlie, arrived to escort the funeral procession to Caney Head. His sheriff's car was shiny-clean and he kept the rotating yellow light flashing. He was wearing a business suit and had left his gun back at the office. Later, he said that Mayhayley's funeral was just a typical Heard County funeral, except for the very large crowd. Clara did not agree for she had been there from the beginning and he had not!

Sheriff Bledsoe pulled his car in front of the hearse and turned on his siren. It made a sad, mournful wail, as the sheriff began the procession on its three-mile trek down the narrow, dirt road.

Clara said that Mayhayley rode that day as never before. Rather than trudging down Caney Head Road to the church with Sallie and several dogs following her, she was riding in a long, black vehicle. Some of her neighbors, without transportation, stood in their yards and watched her slowly ride by in all her glory. Instead of the maypop blossoms and wild flowers she usually carried to Caney Head, today she was surrounded with roses, carnations, gladioli, tinted chrysanthemums, and even orchids. Awaiting her at the church were county officials, bank presidents, wealthy merchants and businessmen with their wives, and members of her favorite profession, the lawyers. All of this attention would have made her proud. Or did.

The large crowd outside the church surged forward upon hearing the sheriff's siren. Nearer and nearer the long procession came, moving ever slowly. The sheriff led the hearse up to the door of the church, right into the crowd, and stopped right in front of the church steps. While the flowers from the house, which had been stuffed in the hearse, were being carried to the graveside, the family members sat and waited in their parked cars.

The nephew-pallbearers moved the heavy casket with its blanket of colorful flowers up the steep steps that reached to the left door of the church, the door traditionally used by only the male members in the "olden days." The casket would later exit the right door, formerly the women's entrance.

Mayhayley's family climbed from their cars and followed the casket into the church. The congregation stood and watched as the casket was rolled down the aisle and eased into place before the long, high bank of flowers that stretched from one side of the church to the other. They remained standing until the entire family was seated.

Mayhayley was home. She had joined this church when she was young, as did her mother before her. She was the one who had begun the practice of burying her family at Caney Head Church rather than with the other Lancasters and the Bassetts, her grandmother's family, in the cemetery deep in the woods near their original log cabins.

She was joining her father and mother, her sister Lucy, her brothers Charles and Bennie. They were resting beneath similar tombstones that she had bought many years ago.

Familiar hymns, accompanied by a new piano, filled the air. All three preachers spoke, which made the service extremely long. Eventually, Mr. Stutts, the funeral director, opened the casket lid for the one last time. He motioned for those sitting on the left side of the church to come forward to view the body, a standard Southern ritual. When they had returned to their seats, the right side of the church formed an orderly line and they, too, moved toward the casket as the pianist softly played. As an act of courtesy to the hundreds who were unable to get a seat inside, Mr. Stutts walked down the left aisle to the open door of the church and motioned for those outside to come in to view the body, if they wanted to. They eagerly accepted his invitation and silently filed through the church, looked, and swiftly returned to the churchyard.

The family came last. One by one they approached the casket and looked at Mayhayley. Most cried, Sallie more than the others. Johnnie, her devoted son, led her back to her seat, the picture of a broken-hearted woman. Finally, the nephews came forward again and rolled the closed casket down the aisle, lowered it down the steep steps, and slowly moved it toward the waiting grave. Another service followed at the graveside.

Mayhayley was buried right beside the well-traveled road, next to her mother, whose epitaph read, "Precious Memories of Mother Will Live Forever." Mayhayley had already selected a very special epitaph for herself.

When the graveside service ended and the casket was lowered into the $110-concrete vault, most of the family members returned to their cars and like the empty hearse, were driven away. Some of the large crowd stayed and watched as shovels of hard, clay dirt were thrown on the lid of the vault. Some took blossoms from the graveside floral sprays to keep as mementos. Clara saw one person take a whole wreath of red carnations. "Oh, well, they would die anyway," she thought.

Lovic took it hard; he had come to care for Mayhayley. Clara would never forget watching her die. And from her prominent seat, as one of the preachers' wives, she had seen the whole funeral service, close up, and enjoyed telling the story of Mayhayley's funeral.

Poor woman, Clara thought. She had never been pretty, in fact, she actually had been disfigured by the rock that flew up and knocked out her left eye when she was young—or was it an umbrella that poked out her eye? Clara didn't know which. She had also heard it happened while Mayhayley was out plowing. She just did not know the truth of it.

"Oh, well, she'd done the best she could with what she had, which was a mite near better than most people did," said the preacher's wife.

CLARA HEARD BRYAN *was a resident of Heard County and the wife of a Baptist preacher who served several churches in Heard and surrounding counties. Though not related to Mayhayley, she was close to the Lancaster family and was a witness to many episodes in Mayhayley's life as well as her death. Clara, is the aunt of Ms. Moore and was very helpful to her as she interviewed Mayhayley's relatives and neighbors. She was born February 8, 1909, and died September 13, 1991.*

6

Looking at Skeletons in the Closet

MARY SAT DOWN IN A LADDER-BACK CHAIR ON THE FRONT PORCH OF her own house. She was exhausted. Everything on her body seemed to hurt — her head, her back, all the way down to her feet — but there was a sense of relief in all those pains because she could finally rest and not worry any more about her sister. It had never been easy being so closely related to Mayhayley Lancaster. During the past two days, though, Mary had been thinking that all the family troubles over Mayhayley's peculiarities had been buried with her at Caney Head Methodist Church Cemetery. She had been wrong.

"All those stories can now be put to rest," Mary had told her children, on the day of the funeral. That Tuesday, she would never forget the date—May 22nd—she had rubbed her stockinged feet against each other again and again. They had been cramped too long in high-heeled, Sunday shoes. They were not fit for walking across a level floor, much less standing up on the clean-swept, barren graveyard while hundreds of people, most of them strangers, walked by Mayhayley's fresh grave. She had been friendly to them, but that was all. As soon as it was respectable, she got in a car and somebody brought her on home.

Mary leaned back in the chair and closed her eyes. She had felt as though the weight of the world had been on her shoulders for days — years, really — and it had just now begun to lift, she had hoped. And NOW this!

101

Mary was the youngest child in the family, but somehow she had always found herself in charge of things. The thought of her sisters and brothers brought to Mary's mind an image of one of her brothers, Bennie—Benjamin Franklin Lancaster. While he had died during World War I, he had not died *in* the war. Despite the rumors otherwise, it was not his ratty old hat that Mayhayley had been wearing all these years. Bennie was not able to go off to any War. He was so badly retarded he would never have qualified for service. He did go to school with Mary and their sister, Nancy, down at Frolona. He was not there to learn, just to be kept. While the other children did their lessons, Bennie sat in the screenless schoolhouse window catching big horse flies, popping them in his mouth, and swallowing them, whole! Mary recalled how Bennie had embarrassed her until she realized that all her classmates did not really care, and thought he was amusing. She learned to join in the laughter, but it was her first realization that her family was a little different from the others in Heard County.

They came from good, solid stock. She remembered many times hearing her parents and other family members correct the pronunciation of their name. "It's Lank'-a-ster, like in England, not Lan-cas'-ter, as Georgia country folks say," they insisted. In this and many other ways, the Lancasters were no different from the rest of the families who lived in this rural county. They sprang from European immigrants who had come here for a better life, and the Lancasters and others had found just that, despite the hardships they had endured. Mary's great-grandmother, Mahala, for whom Mayhayley was named, had forged her own way and amassed quite a fortune in land. The land where Mayhayley and Sallie lived was a part of her family's legacy from their grandfather Lewis's hard work and diligence at the Lancaster Mill. Mary had to admit it was sister Mayhayley who, in recent decades, had built up a valuable estate. No doubt, soon it would be partly hers, she had thought. That is, until what happened today.

Mayhayley often brought disagreeable attention to the family. During the previous year, Mayhayley had been the cause of serious strife among the family members. The rift began when some of the family thought Mayhayley was insane and tried to have her committed. They had good reason to think it because Mayhayley, who was always prone to oddness, had become even more eccentric and downright foolish in the past few years. In the end, a circuit judge in Carrollton had not believed them and Mayhayley was triumphant once again. It played out with Sallie's son receiving a large tract of land, the John Bledsoe place, which Mayhayley had bought when the Hemmings lived there.

Outlandishness was Mayhayley's trademark, though it had not been obvious to Mary in her early years for Mayhayley was already teaching school when Mary was born. During Mary's infancy and early childhood, Mayhayley was beginning to tell fortunes all over west Georgia and east Alabama. Mary vaguely remembered the time Mayhayley left Georgia with a traveling carnival to tell fortunes all across the United States.

She knew Mayhayley had been a politician and involved in the legal profession, though just how involved was up for debate. Mary questioned whether Mayhayley had actually practiced law early in the teens and early twenties, since women could not even vote at that time in Georgia or much of anywhere else in the United States until 1920! She knew that Mayhayley claimed to have been a lawyer and ran a political ad in the "News and Banana," as everyone in these parts called *The News and Banner*, calling herself an "attorney." Regardless of what other people said or what the real truth was, Mary was sure of one thing—Mayhayley believed she was a lawyer!

Money from Mayhayley's many endeavors, whether she was an attorney or not, made it possible for her to buy the family's homeplace after their father died in 1919. It was the first of many pieces of land Mayhayley acquired through the years. Cousin Watson Lancaster told everybody that Mayhayley also got money (once he said $10,000 and another time, $13,000) for defending Leo Frank in the famous Atlanta murder case of 1913. Mary doubted Mayhayley had defended Frank. She believed that Mayhayley may have been hired as a psychic to hunt down the real killer of "Little Mary Phagan," but that was all.

Watson made her mad anyway. He was a first cousin and ought to have had some family loyalty, but she knew that Watson went around the countryside saying Mayhayley was "just out for the money" and didn't know anything about telling fortunes! "What did he know?" Mary wondered.

In the early years, everyone in the family thought Mayhayley was, well, just Mayhayley. She apparently had been born differently. Mary remembered that strangers came over to their house and asked her Mama how Mayhayley got to be the way she was. Her Mama told them that she had always been different. "Just different" was all she would say. Later Mary understood what she meant, as stories abounded about how Mayhayley was "born 'a talking," or "born alive in a cellophane bag." The most popular tale was that she was born with a veil, a caul, or a double veil, as some called it. Mary knew firsthand that the caul story had truth in it. When she was growing up, the "double veil" as they called it, was in a Prince Albert tobacco can that the family kept out in the chicken house, high up on a shelf. Mary had seen it. She had touched it. It was this dried-up piece of something that looked like a pork skin. Sitting on the porch, Mary realized that they probably should have buried it with Mayhayley—that's what superstition said to do. Mary did not even know where it was now and she confessed to herself, that she didn't even look for it. She guessed it had been thrown away after the old house burned and everybody moved away.

Superstitious folk believed that people born with a caul had special powers. Mayhayley believed it, too. Mary remembered Mayhayley told Celestine Sibley, "It's not a learned gift, it's a borned gift. I've got some learning. I taught school. I passed the bar in Carroll County and could practice law, but seeing the future is my art." Mayhayley just loved talking to the newspaper folks. Not her, Mary said to herself.

When she was six or seven, her powers were already well developed, Mayhayley once told a reporter. Family history had it that Mayhayley told her parents that if her older brother, Charles, found a store-bought doll for her she would tell them where to go in the faraway West in order to return with the embalmed body of another brother. Mayhayley also told reporters that her father would often take her behind the chimney and ask her advice on how to run his farm. That was what Mayhayley said. Mary was too young to remember if it was true or just malarkey.

Mary knew one thing for sure — Mayhayley's talent was not evil. Some people called Mayhayley a witch, but Mary knew better. Mayhayley had joined the Caney Head Methodist Church when not much more than twelve years old. She walked to that church, and sat on the front row every Sunday of her life.

In the summer of 1954, at a revival at the Veal Baptist Church, she had found herself defending her older sister's gifts. A visiting preacher started talking about the devil and witches and what the Bible says about sorceresses, and then he said, "You know more about witches than I do, since I heard you have a witch living right here in this county!"

Mary had been flabbergasted. She knew right off he was talking about Mayhayley and there she was, sitting right there among her own people and hearing him saying that her own sister was a witch! She stood up and said, "You don't know nothing about what you're saying. I know exactly who you're talking about and you're bad wrong. She is a fine Christian woman. She goes to church every Sunday, reads her Bible everyday, and knows the Scriptures." After the unexpected retort, Mary sat back down. Not a soul said anything back to her, then or later. Mayhayley never heard what the revival preacher had said about her. She didn't like many preachers anyway and would have dealt with him if she had known about it! So Mary kept it to herself. Fortunately for the preacher, so did every one else.

As Mary sat on the porch, she continued recalling the previous few days, weeks, months and years. Her sister Sallie, had been with Mayhayley the most through these years and it was Sallie's son, Johnnie and daughter-in-law, Evie, who had been at the house that Friday, the 20th. The house they were living in was practically new, having been built in 1954 after the old family house burned to the ground. Rumor had it that one of the family members had set the fire because they were sick and tired of seeing the old hovel on what they hoped would be their place when Mayhayley died.

Regardless, when the call came from Sallie, Mary called Nancy in Carrollton and they and their families promptly came to Mayhayley's bedside. Mary knew Sallie could not look after Mayhayley when she was sick. She never had, really. When things turned really bad for the two older sisters, they always called in Mary or Nancy to save them and Mary had grown "sick and tired" of it.

Mary also knew that most everyone who saw Sallie thought she was some kind of an angel. Mary had to admit Sallie was pretty, that is, if she fixed herself up. Sallie also knew how to keep her mouth shut out in public, so she appeared to be the devoted sister. Behind closed doors, she fought and scrapped with Mayhayley. Some folks who knew the family before Mary was born swore it was Sallie who jabbed out Mayhayley's eye with a stick. That did not surprise Mary when she first heard it.

Mary let a smile crawl over her usually dour face as she recalled the time Mayhayley hired the Lipham photographer from Walnut Hill to come over to their house and take a picture of the whole family. This was in 1904 when brother Charles had come home from Oklahoma for a visit. Mayhayley put her and Nancy and Bennie on the front row where everybody could see them. She put Mama and Papa right behind them. Mayhayley put herself right up front posing with a guitar and she got Charlie Lancaster, a cousin, to pretend he was playing a fiddle. Mayhayley had stuck Sallie on the back row in a corner where nobody would see her. It made Mary chuckle right out loud just thinking about that!

When Sallie came back after living for a while with Johnnie and Evie in Roanoke, a couple of years ago, things became different. Mary found herself writing checks and paying bills and going back and forth, taking both older sisters to doctors and seeing that they had medicine, food, and heat. Mary had enough work running her own big house, but looking after them had left her plain worn out. During the period, Mary was becoming convinced Sallie was out to get all of Mayhayley's money, all fourteen tracts of her land, not counting all the store buildings and houses she owned. Mary had some proof of it from a letter Sallie wrote to Earl Staples, a lawyer up in Carrollton. She had asked him to find out how it was that Mayhayley owned the Lancaster home place, implying that it should have been shared with all eleven Lancaster children. Mr. Staples wrote Sallie back and told her how Mary's own husband, Marvin, had been the administrator of Papa's estate in 1919 and that Mayhayley had bought the farm from him, fair and square, and she could do with it what she wanted. Mary still had that letter.

Sallie was younger than Mayhayley by four years. Mary had come to believe that when Sallie was born, Mayhayley had taken over and looked after her because Mama had so many other children. That was why Mayhayley was always so protective of Sallie, Mary believed. That was the way they had been all their lives: Mayhayley looking after Sallie, but never did Sallie look after Mayhayley! Not once! Sallie did go around with her some and she did herd the customers in and out of the house, but she and Marvin and other family members did that sometimes, too.

In more recent years when Mayhayley was sick, Sallie and Mayhayley would come to Mary's house in Stoney Point or go to Nancy's in Carrollton. Nancy told Mary that no matter how hard she tried to run her house like normal people, the minute Mayhayley showed up, sick or well, a crowd of folk would hear she was there and in no time at all, Mayhayley would have a crowd parked in her yard or standing on her porch and lined up in her front room. Mayhayley did not miss out on seeing any of her customers!

Mary recalled with bitterness how she and Marvin had built a two-room cottage in their back yard for Mayhayley and Sallie to stay in after their old house burned. When Mayhayley saw it, she didn't like it, complained about it, and named it "The Dungeon." Mayhayley wanted to go back home to Heard County, she insisted, as though her house had not burned slap to the ground!

After the family started arriving, word spread rapidly around the county that Mayhayley was bad off and visitors began to come and go throughout the day. Sallie was of no help. She kept calling out for help from anybody. Sallie told Mary, as soon as she and Nancy got there, that no one had called a doctor to see about Mayhayley. Mary said all Sallie did was wring her hands, cry out, and pull at her clothes. Sometimes, Mary said Sallie would go and sit on the bed beside Mayhayley and pat her hand. Mary admitted that at least Sallie could get a response out of their sister. In her own way, sick as she was, Mayhayley would turn her head to look up at Sallie, and sometimes, she would smile at her and mumble something or other.

Saturday night, Mary watched Sallie climb in bed with Mayhayley, both of them sleeping in their day dresses, as if they did not own bedclothes. Mary felt that twinge of embarrassment again, the way she had once felt about Bennie. Most everyone else understood, though, for lots of folk slept in their day clothes, too, she guessed.

When Mayhayley died on Sunday, Johnnie told Mr. Stutts, of Lipford and Stutts funeral home, to give Mayhayley "the very best," which meant the expensive, eighteen-gauge, Wallace-seal, copper-tone casket and to put new clothes on her. Johnnie also asked Mr. Stutts to bring out some flowers if he could get Mrs. McCutcheon to open her florist shop on a Sunday. Mary knew all along that Johnnie was going to pay for all of this with Mayhayley's money, so she just stood around and let him do all the big talk. Mary still had to take over the small details like seeing to the food that was being brought in. She also had to call all the kin, especially those who lived in Alabama and near Atlanta. She charged the calls to the phone on Johnnie's side.

Mary saw to it that the front room was cleared out and the new furniture shoved aside to make enough room for the casket, some flowers, and the crowd that would surely come.

Mary recalled that right before dark, the long, black hearse turned onto the dirt road from Highway 100 and inched among the cars and trucks that were parked all over the road and yard. The hearse found a parking place near the front door of the house. When the hearse arrived everyone in the yard grew silent and stood still. A small group of strong men stepped forward to unload the casket and haul it into the house.

The hushed silence in the yard was broken by the sound of loud shrieking and screaming inside the house. Knowing it was Sallie, she and Nancy ran to the front door to hold her back from the casket. They had expected her to take it hard when Mayhayley's body came back home, but they had not anticipated the fit that Sallie pitched.

In the midst of Sallie's carrying-ons, the casket was brought into Mayhayley's front room and placed against the far wall. Mr. Stutts opened the lid to reveal Mayhayley's face. Her face was visible underneath the thin piece of pinkish gauze which Mr. Stutts draped over the open end of the casket lid. For what one could see through the gossamer, she looked pretty.

The house doors were quickly locked with only Mayhayley and her family inside. Outside, the crowd stayed and seemed to grow bigger. That night more people came and left and some stayed all night. They wanted to see the body; they begged the family. Later, some said the family had been rude to them, shutting down the house like that, but it was the only way the family could have gotten any rest. By midnight all lights were off inside the house except in the front room where two Lancaster men sat up, in shifts, throughout the night beside Mayhayley's casket. It was an old custom known as "sitting up with the dead." A restless crowd also sat up outside and watched for any movements in the house.

Early the next morning, while the families were in the two kitchens cooking breakfast, Mary looked out and saw people already milling around up near the house. She saw one small group band together and start walking toward the kitchen door. Husband Marvin jerked the kitchen door open and demanded to know what they were doing. They wanted to come in and see Mayhayley, they said. "For God's sake," he had shouted back, "it's not even daylight. We haven't even had breakfast yet. Can't you leave us alone? Why don't you go on home and come back about nine o'clock." Then he slammed the door.

The group didn't leave. They just walked back to the cars and stood and waited until 9 o'clock. By that time, the crowd outside was so big even Mary began to feel frightened.

On time, Johnnie unlatched one of the front doors and propped it open with a kitchen chair. A line quickly formed at the door and stretched across the front yard, turned into the side yard, and reached into the backyard—all the way back to the chicken house.

The first person who passed through the doorway was Mayhayley's great niece from Lumber City, Georgia. She bravely walked to the opened casket. There she was: Aunt Mayhayley Lancaster, dressed in a thirty-dollar blue dress with a large purple orchid pinned to the bodice. Her hands were neatly folded across her waist. Makeup had been spread over her face, a light-colored face powder, pink rouge, and a slight touch of pink lipstick. Her thin grayish-brown hair was brushed up away from her face and lifted into a roll on the top of her head. With both eyes closed, even the left one looked normal. She was neat, clean, and orderly, looking no older than her seventy-nine years. In fact, many people said that she looked much younger. One person said that she looked like the prim schoolteacher she once had been.

All day long and into the night, the line came through the front door. Everybody was quiet, yet Mary still sensed that some walked up to the casket with great fear.

Mary came back to the moment, breathing a sigh of anguish. Shortly after the enormous funeral, Mary was horrified to hear that stories were still circulating about her sister and while some were new and totally fabricated, the most common one was that her brain had been pre-sold, long before her death, for a fortune to some hospital in New York. Mary recalled overhearing someone ask Mayhayley if this was true several months before her death. Even with Mary standing right there beside her, Mayhayley did not deny the tale. But Mary knew that there was not a word of truth in it! Had it been true, Mary would have contacted that hospital immediately and told them to come on down, get her sister's brain and bring her a million dollars! Mary also knew that no operation took place at the funeral home in Franklin, for Mr. Stutts had assured her.

The next shock came today when the will was read. After all that she, Nancy, and some of the other family members had done for Mayhayley, the will stated that, except for one hundred dollars to each of the three sisters and one brother, everything went to Sallie. EVERYTHING!

Leaving the Heard County Courthouse after she read Mayhayley's will brought in for probate by the co-executor from Carrollton, Mary had thought, "Can you beat that!"

She had to laugh.

Even in death, Mayhayley was still having her way with their lives.

∾

MARY LANCASTER ARRINGTON was Mayhayley's sister, the last of the family's eleven children and twenty years younger than Mayhayley. Mary was a young child when Mayhayley had already begun to teach school and practice law. As an adult, Mary married and moved to Stoney Point, just over the Carroll County line from Heard County. She was a wife, mother, devoted grandmother, and remained closely involved in her family's affairs throughout her life. She was born June 22, 1895, and died December 6, 1984.

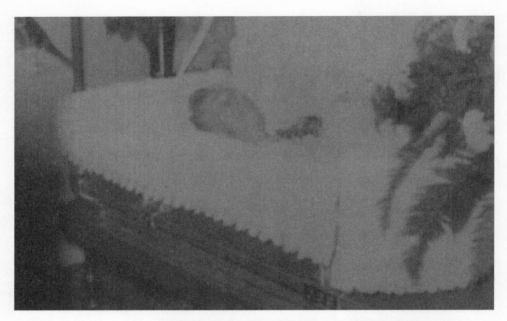

Above, Mayhaley Lancaster in her coffin, May 23, 1955.

Right, Mayhayley's sister, Sallie.

Mayhayley's brothers, Bennie, left, and Charles.

7

Hindsight

Frank Gearreld was an institution on the steps of the county courthouse in Franklin, a living monument in a plain blue serge suit without a tie that paid tribute to the torpid life of Heard County. Gearreld's law office was just around the corner behind the bank and was the only law office in Heard County for many years. His days were calm, writing a few contracts, a divorce now and then, or a land closing every once in a while. Everyone in town knew that he spent more time, later in his life, tarrying on those courthouse steps or inside, than he did at his own desk.

It was a habit he adopted some forty-five years ago when he first came from Newnan to Franklin to practice law with his uncle, Frank Loftin, a revered Confederate veteran and former judge, who was running for the state senate. Young Gearreld soon found that there were few distractions in rural west Georgia and he adjusted. He also discovered that the slow pace of life and his practice of law here meant he could spend many hours loitering and still afford to live in one of the nicest houses in town. Many Southern lawyers enjoyed this leisurely life that included hunting and fishing. Mr.Gearreld did not hunt nor fish.

Though Gearreld was not a native of Heard County, he quickly came to know just about every one of the three hundred or so people who lived in Franklin. He also knew most of the people tucked in the hills around the county seat.

One day, in late summer of 1973, Gearreld was enjoying the breezes and greeting passers-by, when he became curious seeing a strange pickup truck pull up to the curb a few feet away from where he was standing. He was a little surprised when a flustered young man, probably in his mid-twenties, got out of the vehicle and briskly walked up to him at a pace that was rarely used in Heard County. The man did not look the least bit familiar to Gearreld. He had no visage of any long lost son or grandson from some old Heard County family.

"You live around here?" the young man asked without so much as offering his hand for Gearreld to shake.

"Yes sir," Gearreld replied, in a slow drawl, sticking his own hand out to demand the small, polite decency from this impertinent kid. "I'm Lawyer Gearreld."

The young man looked down at Gearreld's extended hand and took it, shaking it in a fast, cursory manner, and then said, "I'm James Wheeler. It's my first year to teach down here at Unity School."

"You seem upset," said Gearreld, clapping the man on the shoulder with his free hand. He still held James's hand in his own tight grip. A firm handshake can say a lot about a man and Gearreld wanted to make sure this youngster knew who was boss.

The young teacher wrested his hand away from Gearreld's and said, "Well, I am a little weirded out."

Gearreld, miffed that the man had escaped his grip, cringed at that terminology. "Young people these days had no grasp of the English language," he thought to himself. "They use these crass phrases when they could say things much more eloquently." Gearreld wondered what kind of education this man was giving the children of Heard County.

"What seems to be the problem?" Gearreld asked.

"I'm trying to find out anything I can about this Mayhayley Lancaster. You can't imagine what happened last night!" Then he added, "Did you know her?"

Gearreld cringed almost visibly at the mention of that name. Did he know her? That was about the most inane question that anyone could ask of any Heard Countian. Of course he knew her, as did everyone else, and, some, like Gearreld, would just as soon have forgotten her. He had not thought of her very much in fifteen years, since he helped settle her estate back in 1957. He had been just as happy to put her out of his mind.

Gearreld did not say what he was thinking. Instead he responded, "Why yes, I knew Miss Mayhayley. What do you need to know about her?" One of Gearreld's latest diversions in life was to keep up with the genealogical court records of people in the county and he liked guiding visitors to the right sources of their family history when they came wandering up to him on the sidewalk or steps. This young man was obviously not a relative of Mayhayley, but Gearreld decided that this would be a good chance to educate this brash teacher about the real Amanda Mayhayley Lancaster.

"I just need to know anything I can about her," James said, a little evasively.

Gearreld smiled. "I'll be glad to help you out," he said, steering the young man to a bench on the sidewalk that was partially shaded by a giant oak tree.

"Is there anything in particular you want to know?" Gearreld asked, once they were settled. The teacher did not seem equipped to take notes or anything, but he was obviously imbued with a strong sense of wonder as well as tension. Gearreld smiled to himself. He had a captive audience.

"How well did you know her?"

As Gearreld had all the time in the world, with nothing to do until he went home for dinner, he cleared his throat, rared back on the seat, and began.

He told the young man that he had heard of her as soon as he moved to Heard County back in the early twenties. He had been taken aback when his uncle told him that the crazy woman who was running against him claimed to be a lawyer. No one had ever proven that she had taken the bar exam, much less passed it, but that didn't stop her from proclaiming her lawyering ability or from using it to gain status in the county and in west Georgia and over in Alabama. Hell, she had even told folks in Atlanta that she was a lawyer. He heard that from Wayne P. Sewell, an old acquaintance of his from up at Roscoe in Coweta County. Sewell said that he had seen her in Atlanta where she was involved in a case at the Capitol. Sewell believed everything Mayhayley said, or so Gearreld had heard.

Gearreld recounted stories of when Mayhayley first ran for office. That was how, in part, he came to Heard County. Mayhayley was running against his uncle, who was seventy-nine years old at the time. His uncle had been astounded to read that the *LaGrange Graphic* had endorsed her and Mayhayley was spreading a story that a well-connected industrialist was backing her!

It seems that Mayhayley had promptly registered to vote in 1922 and was running her first political campaign. Dr. J. C. Taylor was running for the same state Senate seat. When Mayhayley qualified, on August 22, 1922, she became the first woman to seek public office in Georgia, according to records (or lack of records) in the Georgia Secretary of State's office. "That is some kind of record," Gearreld admitted.

"In the fall election Loftin and Taylor split six hundred votes between them and Mayhayley only got thirty-five! Then Uncle Frank won the run-off. And that's how I got here," Gearreld explained. "You might say, Mayhayley brought me!"

Nevertheless, two years later, she paid another twenty-five dollar qualifying fee and ran for the Georgia Assembly, or House, as some called it. After a second loss, Mayhayley ran an ad thanking her voters and blaming her loss on the Ku Klux Klan, which she said, campaigned against any woman! This could have been true, Gearreld told the young man, even though he did not know, firsthand, for he had never belonged to the Klan.

In 1928, she ran for the Georgia Senate again. Her opponent that time was a Dr. Mickle. He received 575 votes; she got 92.

"Some folks still believe she served in the Georgia legislature, which, if true, would make us look like a bunch of fools, if you ask me," Frank Gearreld said.

Gearreld believed she ran for office just to attract attention to herself. Her colorful dress and reputation drew many out to see her as she campaigned around the county in an open-topped Model A automobile, driven by her young cousin, Pearl. That was the point, Gearreld said, to try to get people's attention.

She also challenged her opponents to open debates. All ignored her except his Uncle Frank who appeared at her town meeting. She spoke to small groups of supporters and larger audiences of curiosity seekers with equally great flourish. The campaigns brought more customers up to her house to get their fortunes told! That was what she was really doing, Gearreld was convinced. She was just drumming up business. However, the women in the community did not all agree.

While most rural elections were won by how many folks the candidate knows, how big the family is, and the high voter turnout if the weather is good, Mayhayley ran her campaigns quite differently. She got herself up an actual platform. She proudly published her platform in the newspapers.

In her public notices, she advocated better educational advantages for all children, meaning blacks and whites, and a uniformity of school textbooks. She said she favored "the ladies of Georgia having a right to go to the polls without a heavy poll tax."

"Well, if the women were so all fired-up to vote, why should they not pay poll taxes like everybody else?" Gearreld sputtered.

"She wanted elected legislators to avoid influences of lobbyists during legislative sessions. Now, I've been in the Legislature, young man, and lobbyists are a very valuable commodity!" Gearreld added. "Why, she even favored the Federal reserve system to regulate banks, as if she knew anything about banks! We have to admit though that it was an act yet to come! And, naturally, she wanted more funds for Georgia's rural farm roads.

"Her fifteen-point platform ended with making it a law that all doctors had to answer calls in case of birth because 'the poor can't pay the price.'"

While saying this out loud, Gearreld realized that she had some bright ideas. "Before her time, though," he quickly added.

After her political race in 1928, Mayhayley never ran again, but Gearreld recalled that through the years she continued to speak out on every political issue. She either wrote up her ideas in the local newspaper or just talked about them to anybody who would listen to her.

She supported Roosevelt and even compared him to "a divine entity." She despised Eugene and Herman Talmadge whose established Georgia political machine elected them whenever they ran, yet Mayhayley took every opportunity to criticize them, not a popular position in Heard County, one of the rural counties that always voted for the Talmadges. Once in an interview about her prophetic abilities, a newspaper reporter had asked her age and she replied, "I'll not tell you my age for I'm still planning to run for office again. Maybe this time I can get rid of those blankety-blank Talmadges." When he read the news story, Gearreld knew that she had not said "blankey-blank," but that was what the reporter had written in his story. No newspaper would print her actual words of profanity!

Though she had never won the right to make laws, Mayhayley continued to try and influence the laws and the attitudes of the community. In her weekly newspaper article in the *News and Banner*, she spoke out against "demon rum" and wrote that poor children suffered because their daddies drank whiskey. She urged the county fathers to build a factory so the workers would not have to travel so far to work in the textile mills. She urged business leaders to build a railroad into the county. Gearreld had to give her that one, too, for Heard County became known as the only county in Georgia that did not have a single mile of railroad!

One of the most popular publications in Heard County and throughout Georgia during the 1910s and 1920s, was *The Jeffersonian*. It was a monthly magazine published by Georgia's United States Senator Tom Watson. In the magazine, Watson vilified Jews, "niggers," and Catholics. From 1913 until 1915 his editorials screamed for the electrocution of Leo Frank, the Jewish superintendent of an Atlanta pencil factory and the alleged murderer of Mary Phagan, a poor, thirteen-year-old girl who had been a worker in the factory. The murder case had become a celebrated national cause of the early twentieth century and many Southerners boisterously sang, "The Ballad of Mary Phagan." Watson's vitriolic magazine probably affected the outcome of the trial and the lynching of Leo Frank, which upset Mayhayley, according to her outspoken cousin, Watson Lancaster. Mayhayley did not have the same opinions as most Georgians.

Gearreld told the young man that Mayhayley had attacked Tom Watson in her newspaper column, writing, "*The Jeffersonian* magazine is obscene." Mayhayley once showed Carl Simonton, the local postmaster, a newspaper clipping that identified her with the Leo Frank trial, but Simonton could not remember exactly what it said. By 1915, money poured into Georgia to help Frank avoid the death penalty and many psychics and detectives were hired, Gearreld said. Maybe she was hired to locate the killer.

For years, Gearreld had heard Mayhayley stories. While he didn't necessarily believe all of them, he said that he did not know that they were false, either.

He kept the 1930, full-page article about Mayhayley from the *Atlanta Journal*, "Foretelling *Death* With Cards" on his office wall. The article named the girl who told of Mayhayley's prophecy that her friend "had no future." The friend died in a car wreck the night she left Mayhayley's house. To Gearreld, that proved Mayhayley had some psychic skills, but it still did not make her a lawyer, he emphasized.

In fact, playing the devil's advocate, Gearreld often found himself defending Mayhayley. Over at the courthouse, he reminded her critics of the death of Bernice Somebody, who was also killed in a car accident after leaving Mayhayley's house. How about that other girl who went to her over at Flat Rock Methodist Camp Grounds? "Didn't ol' Mayhayley tell her, too, that she didn't have any future and she'd better watch her step." That was the story Mort Lipford, a Franklin buddy of Gearreld's, told until his own death. Mort said he was there when Mayhayley appeared in an automobile and rode through the campgrounds, which was not allowed, though Mayhayley did it anyway.

"When Cousin Pearl finally stopped the car," Mort said, "she started her own parade! She walked around the huge, ancient arbor in a get-up made up of a dress that was so short that it showed her knees, which she, or somebody else, had painted red!" According to Mort's story, that night at Flat Rock was the first time Mayhayley had told anybody that they would die or that they had "no future," which meant the same thing to everybody.

Gearreld told the young man that most Franklin people said she was "just a bunch of hokum" and publicly denied ever going to see her, but once something was lost, they sneaked out of town and went her way. She had found their lost hunting dogs, their missing shot guns, and more jewelry than one would think was possessed in a town as small as Franklin!

Still, Gearreld knew her mainly from a distance and insisted that he'd never gone to her for fortunetelling. He saw her in Franklin most "First Tuesdays" when the sheriff's tax sales were conducted. However, if one of the nearby counties also had property tax sales on a first Tuesday that interested her more, Mayhayley might be seen at the Carroll County Courthouse, at the Coweta County Courthouse at Newnan, the Troup County Courthouse at LaGrange, in Randolph County, Alabama, at Wedowee or even at LaFayette at the Chambers County Courthouse.

Unlike most people in the area, she had ready cash. She was lucky at the property sales, too. Gearreld knew that once she had paid $11.17 for a large tract of land that was partly in Heard County and partly in Coweta County. It soon was worth thousands of dollars in timber sales alone! When Gearreld heard that Mayhayley owned it, he said, "Some timber magnate will end up wanting the timber and the land. Her estate will end up making a small fortune." He had been right. In 1956 the eleven dollars, plus change, turned into $30,000!

"You gotta' hand it to her. She knew how to get those superstitious fools' money for herself and then used it to buy everything in sight," he said aloud.

Gearreld said the first time he came face to face in a courtroom with Mayhayley was in 1929. At that time, Mayhayley already owned most of one side of the Franklin Square. She kept a small place in an old house next to the jail to use when she was in town and later she told fortunes in the Alsabrooks home right off the square. Sometimes, if she was not busy at the tax sales, she would set up a small table and drag out a chair, which was all the equipment she needed to tell a few fortunes and pick up twenty or thirty dollars in a short time. "She made big money back for those times," he added.

Mayhayley had come into their law office with a case of her own. Her insurance had expired on the building where the barbershop was located, and there had been a fire, she announced. Her tenant, the barber, was demanding money for his lost equipment. She had promised him the building and its contents were insured when she rented it to him, but now she confessed she was not sure she had paid the last premium on the insurance. Further investigation revealed that she had not paid *any* full premiums! Gearreld and his uncle did not want her case and sent her on to Colonel Willis Smith in Carrollton, also a Heard County native, who was usually very sympathetic and helpful to Mayhayley.

On Mayhayley's behalf, Smith wrote the insurance company a letter but their answer stated that she had only paid small amounts, maybe a dime or a quarter, and the insurance company implied that they were "sick and tired" of her. They not only hoped that she got sued by the barber, but were willing to assist "as a friend of the court." Smith then returned the insurance company's letter to Gearreld's office.

Gearreld recalled the outcome of that case with great delight. Gearreld said he had been standing outside the courthouse when he saw Mayhayley coming. He knew she was in Franklin as a result of Sheriff Charlie Bledsoe's summons. Mayhayley knew that a sheriff-delivered summons meant for her to be there and to be on time.

As Gearreld watched, Mayhayley hurried down the sidewalk in front of the courthouse, and up the broad granite steps that led into the tall, brownstone courthouse. After he saw her enter through the deeply carved, double doors, he, too, strolled up the walk and followed her into the corridor and up the broad inner staircase.

As he entered the courtroom, discreetly behind Mayhayley, Gearreld saw an older, well-dressed, dark-suited man sitting with a similarly dressed younger man, probably his assistant. Gearreld figured they had come to town from Atlanta to represent the insurance company. He wondered how they had gotten in the court-room without his seeing them arrive, then he remembered that he had walked into the Bank of Heard County to cash a small check. Gearreld found a seat for himself by a window while Mayhayley was seating herself in a chair at the defendant's table. She was alone.

The judge gaveled the room to order and the few Heard Countians who were hanging around became quiet. Gearreld heard Mayhayley tell the judge that she was a lawyer and she was representing herself. Gearreld knew that some judges enjoyed

Mayhayley's friendship and had often gone along with her courtroom business. In fact, back in the 1910s, Judge Alva Dean Freeman of Newnan had asked Mayhayley to represent the American Bar Association in a ceremony in this same courtroom. No one knew if it was a joke — Judge Freeman was a renowned teaser and very popular raconteur — or if he really believed that she was a member of that professional association and wanted to honor her in some way. Mayhayley had written up the occasion in the *News and Banner* and kept it with her over the years.

Gearreld watched the proceedings, and as he expected, the barber won the case and Mayhayley was ordered to buy him some new equipment. She whined, shook her head from side to side, and pled with the judge to let her "work it out with the barber." She was, after all, only a poor farm woman and the only caretaker of her widowed mother, she told the judge.

The judge smiled. He knew better. He reminded her of her promise to insure her tenant's equipment and then he ordered her to go to the bank across the street and get the money. He instructed her to return by 5 o'clock because he had to get home. Mayhayley, wearing a dark scowl on her face, left the courtroom as ordered.

Gearreld watched her from one of the large side window of the courtroom as she walked across the town square, not to the bank, but toward her own house by the jail. Her shoulders were slumped forward as she slowly walked. While she was gone, the court continued with the next case. A whiskey agent had caught yet another bootlegger.

Within an hour, Mayhayley reentered the courtroom. She marched to the front, swung open the wooden divider and took her former place at the defendants' table even though there were others sitting there.

"Miss Mayhayley," the judge called out. "Are you aware that you are intruding on this court's demeanor? Don't you know that you do not have the privilege of coming in here and interrupting us, especially noting that you were assigned a later time to return?"

The judge was somber, stern, and appeared angry. Others in the courtroom were smiling, snickering, and showing every sign of amusement, except for laughing out loud. Gearreld often said he would not have missed that show for anything!

Mayhayley, as usual, disregarded any clamor she made. She chunked a large, multi-colored bundle onto the table. Methodically, she turned out each corner of the fabric, which apparently was an old shawl, while she peered into the bundle. The judge could see that her bundle included a morass of coins and dollar bills. Carefully, she picked out bills of large denominations and haphazardly slammed each one on the table. Then, she began to pick out bills of lesser denominations, along with some coins, and tossed them on the table. The courtroom spectators, the defendants, and the lawyers left their seats and gathered around her to watch and to stare into the shawl. Gearreld chuckled aloud just remembering that Mayhayley had lost her case!

In the years to come, Gearreld had other encounters with Mayhayley. He represented the Bank of Heard County, where Mayhayley kept a sizable balance. He was called upon to represent the bank when she sued the bank for allowing a family member to cash checks on her account without her signature. She won that case and Gearreld lost.

When Mayhayley was charged with mental incompetence, Gearreld represented the part of her family that was trying to put her away. Luther Wyatt was his partner. They pressed for her incarceration. They lost; Mayhayley went free. When Mayhayley's will was presented for probate four days after her death, Gearreld represented those family members who were stricken from the will, except for a measly $100. He and Wyatt got them a settlement of $60,000, and he and Wyatt split $13,000 in attorney fees.

Gearreld always said he figured that, as lawyers, he and Mayhayley came out about even. He still held it against her, though, that she had "wiggled out of so many things" and he had been on the losing end of too many of those wiggles. Once her estate had been settled, he sighed to himself and thought good riddance. "That's the end of her messing with this county and my life," he had thought.

Now, sixteen years later, Mayhayley resurfaced, bothering Gearreld. The young teacher was soaking up every word.

"Why do you care about her?" Gearreld finally asked.

"Well, first, my parents always said that she predicted my birth and said that I would be a teacher, years ago when they were newlyweds and honeymooned at Dunaway Gardens. But now something else has happened. Last night some of my students and I were going by Caney Head Methodist Church graveyard where she is buried. It was a bright night, you know what a big moon there was last night, and we could all see the gravestones very clearly. As we rode by her grave, a bright light came down right beside my truck and as we watched, another bright light hit Mayhayley's grave and it just blew up!"

He said he and his students were terrified. Last night, as he dropped the students off at their houses, they went in and told the families what they had seen, but nobody believed them. This morning the children begged him to drive them back up there again and see what they could see. Maybe they had just imagined all of this; at least that was what the parents said last night. He took them back, all loaded up in the back of his truck during their lunch hour and, sure enough, Mayhayley's headstone was toppled forward and broken into two pieces. The bricks that surrounded the graveside were spread out like a fan from the concrete mounting. Mayhayley's slab lay partially hidden by the headstone, but they could see it was cracked in many places.

"I thought maybe somebody could explain all of this. Do you think she was a supernatural person?" the young teacher asked.

Gearreld was thinking. Maybe he and his wife might ride up to Caney Head this Sunday afternoon to see the newly broken grave and the debris, which, he had heard, included beer bottles, pink panties, and empty cigarette packs. Gearreld knew that some of the church members already wanted deputies to patrol the Caney Head Road because teenagers were telling that some (they said they were not the ones, of course) were going up there and "making out" on the slabs.

Gearreld pondered the young man's story. If Gearreld said that he believed the grave really "blew up," everybody in the county might hear about it and think he was going nuts! If he told the teacher his story was crazy and nothing like that could have happened up at Caney Head, how could he account for the broken-up grave? And the truth was, for some strange reason, he believed the young man's version.

"What could have happened up there?" Gearreld wondered to himself. Maybe it was grave robbers. Stories abounded, even before Mayhayley had died, that she had sold her brain to some medical research group so her brain could be examined and maybe they would learn from her gray matter what gave her psychic powers. In fact, he knew of one Lancaster kinswoman who believed that her grave had been opened and that her head removed. The cousin swore that she had seen Mayhayley's head floating in a jug of formaldehyde in a hospital in Atlanta—her hair swishing around if you shook the jug!

All accounts of Mayhayley's burial agreed that her brain went to the grave with her body. Gearreld had been there for the funeral, he recalled.

Gearreld remembered that he had been in his office looking at some land titles the day Mayhayley was being laid to rest. Hugh Mickle, the bank president, pulled himself up the narrow, steep steps to Gearreld's office and asked, "You want to go up to Caney Head to the funeral this afternoon?"

"Not really," Gearreld had replied.

Mickle coaxed him and Gearreld, knowing he had nothing really pressing to do, got up, put on his suitcoat, and followed Mickle out of the office, not even bothering to lock the door. On the way up to Caney Head, Gearreld talked with Mickle about the IRS lien on Mayhayley's bank account and on her property, a lien that had languished in his Mayhayley file for more than four years now. Gearreld remembered thinking that, now that Mayhayley was dead, the lien would have to be settled by her lawyer, and that sure wasn't him! The bank and he would no longer have to worry about that problem.

He remembered thinking, on the day of her funeral, that Mayhayley's will would likely have some surprises. It did. He also remembered thinking that, finally, his life would be free of this bothersome woman who always seemed to crop up and make Gearreld work a bit too hard.

Sitting there with the young teacher, Gearreld wondered if some conniving con artist had decided Mayhayley's brain or body was worth stealing even after all these many years, as a museum piece, not for medical research. Maybe somebody had been up there robbing the grave and that's what the teacher and his students had seen during the lightning flashes. God knows anything was possible when it came to Mayhayley Lancaster. Most likely, though, the thunderstorm tricked their eyes, Gearreld thought. Folk do and see funny things when they are excited or scared.

That was how he tried to explain the exploding grave. "It was probably just the lightning striking that grave," Gearreld said. "After all, Mayhayley had the highest headstone in the graveyard, so it was just asking to be struck. If I were you, I just wouldn't let it worry me at all."

That explanation seemed acceptable to the young teacher and soon Gearreld was sitting alone under the shady oak.

Gearreld began to feel almost hot as the sun shifted West to set. But for just a moment, he felt a chill run over him, that creepy feeling everyone describes as "a rabbit running over your grave." For a brief moment, he wondered if it was Mayhayley, free from her grave, again wandering the streets of Franklin and the back roads of Heard County.

"Naw," Gearreld said out loud, though only to himself.

"Even Mayhayley couldn't wiggle out of that spot."

FRANK GEARRELD was a native of Newnan who moved to Heard County as a young man to practice law with his uncle, Frank Loftin, a revered Confederate veteran, judge, and senator. After Loftin died, Gearreld ran his own private law practice in Franklin. Both Gearreld and his uncle had numerous legal dealings with Mayhayley and her family. He was born April 19, 1901, and died April 23, 1983.

8

Evie Sees it Differently

"SCRATCH, SWISH, SQUEAK, SQUEAK" WENT THE DISHRAG AS EVIE RUBBED the oilcloth-covered kitchen table. While she wrung out the cotton rag that she was tightly squeezing into her kitchen sink, she continued to talk to her three awe-struck visitors. They were sitting in Mayhayley Lancaster's last home where she had died more than twenty years before.

"No, there was absolutely nothing to her. She made up those things and said them over and over. Sometimes when she gave out of new things to say, she'd tell about a "black eyed-girl" all one day, then the next day, she'd be telling about a "dark-haired man." I listened to her, not that I was being snoopy, but I lived in the house with her, and I saw and heard what was going on."

"What did you see?" asked the young lawyer, one of the three who were visiting in Evie Farmer Mitchell's kitchen, the kitchen that had rightly become hers when Mayhayley, Johnnie, and then Sallie died.

"I saw a lot. I mean I saw a lot. I saw those crowds of people—I never saw so many folks in my life that would come here on Sundays. They'd stand around in the yard, dropping papers and trash all over the yard. You never saw so many cigarette butts. Old stinking cigars, too.

"On Sundays, they'd even wait around until Mayhayley and Sallie got home from church. In the last few years, Johnnie, my husband, you know, was taking them over to Caney Head in his pickup and then he had to go back and get them when he figured church was over. But that crowd would wait.

"Johnnie never could tell how long church was going to last, 'cause Mayhayley sometimes hung around at the end and argued with the preacher about the Scriptures and talked to any and everybody who was at Caney Head. Johnnie also waited while she took some kind of old weed-flower to the graveyard to put on her mama and daddy's graves.

"You know, Baptists take a Bible to church, but Mayhayley was a Methodist and they don't do that—leastwise, they don't around here. What she took to church was those dogs! They'd follow her and Sallie if they walked down the road, or they'd jump up in the back of Johnnie's pickup, if they were riding. I'd stand at that very door there and watch them haul-buggy down the road. Those dogs would jump up in the back end of the pickup and would be just a yapping and barking and running around in circles. It's a wonder the cats didn't go too, 'cept cats don't appear to like to ride, but I've never seen a dog that didn't go for air in its face.

"I asked my neighbor, James Bryan, what she did when she got over there to the church but James said he didn't go to that church, but he'd always heard that when Mayhayley and Sallie got there that those dogs would follow them through the church door and go down the aisle, just like they were members! Since Mayhayley always sat on the front seat, probably so she could see, James said he heard that those dogs would hunker down and curl themselves up around her feet and even stretch out in the aisle. That way the dogs could look straight up at the preacher and get a little Methodist religion, whatever that's worth, James had said laughingly.

"I always thought those dogs were about the strangest thing about Mayhayley—the way she had such power over them. Around her, they hardly ever barked unless they were scared, and they never made any noise at all around her unless it was when they scratched themselves. But she could give them a stare and they'd even quit that! But she couldn't keep them from messing in the flower pots and on the porch and in the yard, just everywhere!

"If it wasn't dog mess, then it was cat mess and it stunk up the inside of the house, and chicken you-know-what was everywhere. Y'all don't know what I put up with those animals of hers!"

The remembrance of those experiences were making Evie's face turn red. Because she was a very neat and orderly person, she then wiped her eyes with a neatly folded clean handkerchief that she took from her apron pocket, should her eyes become watery.

"Now if the dogs were following her down the roads, I've heard her yell and holler at 'em. She first called them 'Mutt' and then she'd call them nasty names like 'Black b----' — it rhymes with witch. While the cats didn't go nowhere with her, like go to church, but here at the house those cats followed her around and then they'd curl up near her feet and never move until she moved. Don't you think that's strange?"

After Evie lined up the sugar bowl and salt and the pepper shakers on the kitchen table, she pulled up a chrome and vinyl kitchen chair to her now shiny table and sat down. She stared at her three visitors, mainly addressing her remarks to the young man, a lawyer, that she had known ever since she came to Heard County from Roanoke, Alabama.

"You won't believe this, but I swear I have seen chickens walk all over the backs of the cats and dogs as they lay near her feet. I guess if a rattlesnake came up, it would have laid down besides her feet, too. She had power over animals. I saw it with my own eyes."

"How long did you live with them?" asked the middle-aged reporter who was poised with her pen and paper.

"I'll tell you that when I get through telling you about going to church with the dogs. When church was over, those big, skinny, scrawny dogs would follow her up the aisle and go on out to the graveyard with her. If Johnnie drove off and left the dogs at the church, then they'd run as hard as they could, trying to catch up with her. And somehow, they'd all end up back at the house. Now, ain't that something? You three just tell me if you don't think that's not really something!

"Well, I'd say Sallie lived with me and Johnnie, her boy, when we lived over in Alabama in Randolph County for about two years—off and on. Sallie was special to our own little boy and she liked to play with him and keep him close to her. You understand Sallie was his grandmother and Johnnie was all she had. Then Johnnie came up with the idea of all of us moving to Heard County and taking over for them. After that, I was with Mayhayley all the time for about three years. That's about it, three years."

Evie was not used to visitors, that is, not after Mayhayley died, but the three visitors had called ahead and asked for permission to come. She seemed to welcome the local lawyer, the reporter, and the third one who was a beautiful young lady who was between jobs and visiting around with her friends until something interesting came along. To her, Mayhayley was becoming very interesting.

The three were "on a lark," an expression that Mayhayley often used. She'd explained to her customers that "being on a lark" was a saying about having a good time, because a lark was the only bird that "could sing whilst it flew."

The winter day, December 11, 1976, was cold, dark, and dreary and it had been raining for several days when Evie's visitors arrived. While the main road was now paved and finding the house was easy for the young lawyer, the road up to Evie's was muddy and the car slid a time or two getting up the incline to her house. Even though they were sitting in the neat, clean, dry kitchen, they were very aware of the downpour outside the house.

After the initial questions were asked on that gloomy afternoon, Evie talked and talked, appearing to welcome the opportunity to tell stories about Mayhayley Lancaster.

"It was right after we came over here to live with them that one of the neighbors came by telling about us about Mayhayley finding a body many years before. The drowning had been down at Victory."

"Victory? Where is Victory?" asked the reporter.

"Well, Victory is down near Franklin, over towards LaGrange. The main thing to know is that Victory is close to the Chattahoochee River. Down there, the Chattahoochee is as wide as it ever gets. It's real deep down there, too. And it gets thick as mud after a hard rain.

"And that's what had happened at Victory: a hard rain had got the water up and it wasn't fit for fishing, but you can't tell nobody nothing, so this boy, he wasn't really a boy, but a young man with a wife and children, he left out early on a Sunday morning and said he was going fishing. He didn't come back that day. Then he didn't come back that night. So the next morning his wife went down to her daddy-in-law's and told him that she was worried and asked him to do something.

"So the daddy went off in his john-boat and rode around on the river, but didn't see a thing, so he came on back and got his brother to get his john-boat and they both looked. But they didn't see anything, so the two of them went on to Sheriff Bledsoe and reported the boy missing. Now that message brought a whole gang of men from around Victory to the river and they went up and down the river in motorboats and afoot on the river banks, but they still didn't find anybody. You know what happened next, don't you?

"The daddy came up here and told her the story I just told you. Mayhayley told him that it would have been far better if he had come up there and told her about it right after his boy was missing. If he had come on, they might could have revived him. The next morning she could have seen him clear as day, right there on the Chattahoochee. That's what I heard.

"Hearing that story, I never felt so sorry for a man in my whole life, and Mayhayley just blessing him out about not coming on, like-ways it was his fault that the boy still wasn't found.

"Then I heard that Mayhayley halfway apologized to him and said she was sorry that those children wouldn't have no daddy and they were from a good family and a lot of malarkey like that. The daddy was just sitting there, blowing his nose and wiping his face, and Mayhayley just kept talking on and on. That's what I heard.

"Finally, she stopped fussing at him and making him feel so bad. She told him to get a crew together and get in the river at Franklin and go down the river for about five miles and start looking to the right side of river. Right past where the Hillabahatchee Creek runs into the Chattahoochee, look real close around some tree roots and they'd see him. 'He still has all his clothes on, except for his hat. You'll see his hair, it's kinda' longish, floating around his face and stuck on his eyes. He's there!'

"The daddy left and that would have been all Mayhayley knew except that she saw in the *News and Banner* about them finding his body. Soon afterwards the daddy came back to give Mayhayley some money, since he'd forgot to pay her when he rushed off. First, she took his money, then she gave it back, saying that the children would need it more than she did. Sometimes she would do that, but not often.

"I remember hearing that Jordan Webster, one of her neighbors, was standing in his yard one day when Mayhayley went walking by. Jordon saw her coming and rushed in his poor-looking house, then came out and hollered out to her to wait up. When he walked towards her he was digging in a cigar box and pulling out some one-dollar bills and rooting around for some more money while he was talking to Mayhayley. He was telling her he was sorry that he had had such a hard time paying her for that pair of mules he had gotten from her.

"She was looking at Jordan's house and at his little skinny-looking children standing on the porch in their filthy rags. She told me that she said, 'You damned fool, keep your money, you need it more'n I do.'

"When she told that story to me and I asked her why she called him 'a fool' and she said back to me, 'That's what he is: poor house, poor children, poor farm. That's a fool, if you ask me.' I don't exactly understand that except you gotta' hand it to Mayhayley, she wasn't no fool when it came to money."

While the trio was listening to Evie, they heard some rustling noises around in her house—muffled sounds of doors closing and footfalls on the hardwood floors. An eerie feeling, as though Mayhayley was somewhere about and maybe listening in on their conversation—it settled down onto all three of them at once. Noticing the discomforting change in her guests's expressions, Evie quickly recognized their demeanor and put their minds to rest. She explained that the noises were from her son and his family who were now living in the other side—Mayhayley's side—and that they were a comfort to her since she didn't like living alone.

"You know this house had two sets of rooms, a duplex is what they call it and the best thing about it for us is that it has two complete kitchens and two bathrooms.

Why they put a big nice, white bathtub on Mayhayley's side, I'll never know, for neither one of them would get near a bath.

"Once when Mayhayley was in some trouble with the law and was having to go to the courthouse, she was wearing a dress that had mud all over it—the mud was caked on the hem— and it made a clunking noise when she walked. I asked her if she wouldn't want to sort of 'spiff up' before she went to see the lawyers. She didn't answer me but I followed her into her bathroom and watched her pull up the hem of her dress and swished it around in the sink and then wring the dirty water out into the sink. The tail of her dress was sopping wet and there was dirt still in the sink when I saw her pull that glass eye out of her face and kinda' swish it around in the sink, too. In that same dirty water!

"And then while I was watching her, she pried open that eye socket and stuck the false eye in her face! I swear, I saw her do it. Then she said that she was ready to go up to Carrollton and she dripped on out of the house!

"Sallie, you know, that's my mother-in-law, she called the new bathtub 'a pig trough.' And she didn't like to take baths, either. She cursed and called me and Johnnie really bad names when we stripped her off and tried to give her a bath. Some of the time, Sallie talked as bad as Mayhayley, so even with the two of us tugging and pulling on her, we never did get her in that bathtub. Like I said, it was a bad waste of money buying that bathtub, but now with my family living there, I am proud to say that they use it a lot. They are just as neat and clean as they can be—I think that comes from good raisin', if you ask me."

"Anything else you want to tell us before we go down to LaGrange to see Luther Wyatt?" the lawyer asked.

"I guess you've been to see Lela Ridley about those poisonings, haven't you?"

"What poisonings?" the reporter burst out.

"Lela Persons is her real name. She tells this story right because she was a friend of Lent Hicks, whose family got poisoned. It seems Lent's sister, his brother-in-law, and one of their grandchildren got real sick and were getting worse and worse. The family didn't have any idea of what was wrong with them—it was mainly "vomicking" that wouldn't stop. So Lent came up here and told Mayhayley that he wanted her to help him see about them. There wasn't a colored doctor here in Heard County—still isn't—and since they were colored maybe they needed a little help to get a white doctor to come, I guess he came here too because Mayhayley had a reputation of not turning colored folks away. But mainly, he wanted to know what was wrong down at his sister's and to see if she could get him some help.

"Lela's story is that after Lent told Mayhayley what was going on down at the house and how one of the teachers that was boarding with them had already died, Mayhayley just sat real still and quiet-like until she busted out and said that they were getting poisoned by well water.

"Now this is the strange part: Mayhayley went on and told Lent that he had to go home to his sister's house as fast as he could get there for she could see two children carrying some more well water into the house—she could see it plain as anything—and that he'd better hurry home and grab that water away from those children.

Evie explained to her three visitors that Mayhayley told him, "Throw that bucket of water on the ground in the yard, then call a horse over—a horse will be standing in the yard by a chinaberry tree. That horse won't drink that water, as thirsty as it is."

"That's exactly what happened," Evie continued. "When Lent got to his sister's house, he looked up to see those two children taking a bucket of water up the steps. Mayhayley had even told Lent their names. It was just like Mayhayley said it would be! And that the horse would not drink that water, either.

"Lent got a jar of the well water, and Grady Ridley, a neighbor, took the jar to Atlanta and the report said it was water poisoned with arsenic. 'Course they boarded up the well and the man who was doing the poisoning was arrested and died in jail before they could hang him!

"If it hadn't been for Mayhayley telling Lent about the water, there's no telling how many more people would have died."

"How many people ended up dying?" asked the reporter.

"Four in all. Lela went to the funeral where three of them were buried together over at New Hope Baptist Church."

"Anything else? " the reporter questioned.

"Well, to end it all, I'll tell you what I saw with my own two eyes. It happened right after we got here and we were all staying down in the hollow in an old, really bad house. You know, Mayhayley's log cabin was burned up by somebody, and I know who it was, but I am not telling.

"Anyway, I was in the back of the shack fixing us some supper, when I heard thunder. I figured the thunder was real far off. I was wrong. In just a minute, I heard the biggest clap of thunder I ever heard in my life! It nearly knocked me off the floor, it was so loud. Then a near blinding streak of lightning shot right through that house! I was cooking on a wood stove or I guess I would have been dead.

"Since I'd already heard that Mayhayley was scared of storms and sometimes ran out of the house when a storm was coming up, I rushed over to the front room where Mayhayley was sitting with a whole crowd of people. They were inside the house waiting to have their fortunes told. Maybe they had seen the storm coming up and had come on into the house, I never thought of that until now, maybe, that's why there were so many people in her room and not outside where you were supposed to wait.

"When I got to her door, I saw her jump out of her chair and run toward the outside door. While she was running, I saw her fling that Army hat on the floor and grab a sunbonnet that was hanging on a nail by her door. I followed after her to see where she was going and I saw the whole thing I'm telling you about. Most everybody else in the room also crowded about the door to see what in the world was going on when she just upped and ran out of the room.

"She tore out into the yard and went to this old half-dead cedar tree. She commenced to hitting that tree with her sunbonnet. She was whaling the stew out of the tree and then I heard something that you won't believe.

"She was yelling, 'G— D— Ron George. G— D— Ron George,' and she was not saying 'G— D—' she was shouting out the real thing! Over and over, she was yelling and screaming and beating that tree. The rain had started by the time she got to the tree and now the raindrops were beating down on her as hard as nails, but she just kept on cursing and beating the tree. I was so embarrassed to hear all those words. And then Ron George—he was our neighbor at the time—he was such a nice man and I never knew why she chose him to pick on at that particular moment, but she did.

"Then, just as suddenly as it started, that rain stopped. It just passed on over the yard as fast as any thunderstorm I ever saw move. The rain was *all* stopped! Already there were little puddles standing in the yard and she was still standing out there soaking wet.

"As calm as you please, she turned herself towards the house and walked real slow back to us. She looked tired. She had that soaked sunbonnet dripping from her hand when she came back into the room and then she just dropped it on the floor. I mean she dropped that wet, wringing wet thing on the floor and it lay there, getting stepped on until I slipped back in there and picked it up and washed it out.

"All of us who had been watching her, we just went back to our places. Somebody handed her the Army hat and she perched it on her head and sat back down again.

"When everybody was gone away that afternoon and Mayhayley was still smelling damp, I went back into her room and told her that everybody was gone from outside. She nodded, yet still sat in her old chair.

"I couldn't help it, but I asked her, 'What was all that tree hitting and cursing about? I never saw or heard anything like that before even when I lived over in Alabama. What was all that about?' I asked her again.

"She looked up at me and said as plain as I am talking to you, she said, 'That's how I stop rain.'"

That story could not be topped.

They were all silent for a moment, then the reporter asked a question that all three guests probably wanted to hear answered.

"Miss Evie, looking back on it, twenty-five years later, what do you think of all of this?"

Evie quickly replied, "Like I said at first. 'She made it up!'"

"But she did find the body at Victory, didn't she?" the reporter countered.

"Oh, yes, she knew exactly where it was. I believe that she told the daddy where to find his son. It's in the paper if you want to go read it."

"Did she make up the arsenic poisoning down at Lent's sister's house? Didn't you say she saw those children taking that bucket of poisoned water up the steps?"

"That's right. She did. But then maybe somebody told her about it!"

"Before it happened, somebody told her about it? Who could have done that?" the reporter asked.

"Everybody down there knew that there were two men who were running around with the same woman—anybody could have suspected something bad would happen."

"How about stopping the rain? Did that really happen?" asked the lawyer.

At this, Evie bristled, "Are you doubting what I saw with my own eyes? I saw that rain stop with my own eyes! I saw her bring in that sunbonnet and drop it in the floor and I washed it out myself. I washed it out clean and hung it on the line my own self!"

Obviously, it was time to change the subject for the reluctant hostess was clearly getting hostile.

To change the mood in the room, the lawyer asked, "Miss Evie, did you go to the funeral? Did you go and see all those celebrities and hear the music? Wasn't that a day? I can tell you, I'll always remember it!"

There was a long, long pause. Evie's face fell. She initially appeared shamed, but then a defiant resolve came across her face as she clenched her fist and stood and stared hard at the lawyer.

"To tell it all, I didn't go. Those undertakers had left skid marks on the floor when they wheeled out the casket. Pieces of flowers and fern leaves were strewn all over the floor. Wadded up Kleenexes were laying on the chairs and dirty dishes were strewn all over my kitchen. Somebody had to clean up this mess. That somebody was me!"

"Scratch, squish, squeak, squeak" were the last sounds the trio heard as they quietly left Mayhayley's house in the horrendous downpour.

Where was Ron George when they needed him?

❧

EVIE FARMER MITCHELL was Mayhayley's niece-in-law and the wife of Sallie's son, Johnnie. Though she and Johnnie lived for many years in Roanoke, Alabama, they visited the Lancaster family often and Sallie lived with the couple and their young son for a year in Roanoke. In 1952, three years before Mayhayley's death, Evie, Johnnie and their young son moved to Heard County to live with Sallie and Mayhayley and serve as their caretakers. Evie was born September 5, 1908, and died August 5, 1994.

Epilogue

Last Sight

THE LAST TIME I SAW MAYHAYLEY WAS ON ANOTHER DECORATION DAY, the first Sunday in May of 1954. We had been through the service, visited the cemetery, and stuffed ourselves at the dinner-on-the-grounds. I rode with my father and his pretty second wife up to see Mayhayley's newly constructed house, which was about two miles from the church. As usual, she was glad to see Daddy. She bragged about her new house which had a hardwood floor. Mayhayley said about the floor, " . . . you couldn't put a pin through it." I am sure she was recalling the days when she had peered through the cracks in her floor and watched chickens, cats, and dogs ramble underneath her old log house.

Daddy told her that I was still a single girl and an English teacher in Bessemer, Alabama. Mayhayley reminded him that she had taught my grandmother years ago over at Red Oak School, around the turn of the century. She could not remember the exact year. I remember that Mayhayley seemed very happy that day, and so were we. It was a wonderful, last memory.

The following year in 1955, I did not attend Decoration Day. I had married and was teaching English, speech, and drama at Sidney Lanier High School in Montgomery. I was also pregnant and sick as a dog. I didn't make it to Decoration Day nor to Mayhayley's funeral, which occurred just two weeks after Decoration Day. I never saw her again, but she has never left me, either.

Was Amanda Mayhayley Lancaster all she claimed to be? What of her claim to clairvoyance: "The Oracle of the Ages?"

Well, I believe her. I believe her gift of seeing into the future to be genuine. This should not astound anyone nor is it of any great matter. From time immemorial, civilizations have included those who walked among them with this inexplicable talent and many have been believed with far less evidence than Mayhayley had proffered. Solely because we belong to the Age of Technological Science, and fail to prove, scientifically or clinically, what some do not understand, is a flimsy basis for disbelief.

I have my own reasons to believe.

My older brother has a story about Mayhayley, which I did not hear until several years into my research. Apparently, months before I first remember seeing Mayhayley in the Macedonia Baptist Church cemetery, a young family was going up to Heard County to visit relatives. They were riding up the Frolona Road nearing the iron bridge that spanned the Hillabahatchee Creek. They had been off the paved road for many miles and were moving more slowly as Frolona Road got hillier and more narrow. As they crossed the bridge, they passed through the deep shade of the heavily canopied creek passage. They could see up the creek to the waterfalls and the immense, granite boulders that sprayed the fern-laden bank with mist.

Ferroll Sams, a gifted Georgia writer who also knew the area of Hillabahatchee Creek, once described the creek area as rich with plant and animal life. He said the area is profuse with cardinal flower, galax, lilies of all kinds, azalea, sweet shrub, bluets, blood root, witch hazel, chinquapin, mountain laurel, and all sorts of other rooted things. Teeming among these plants and the rocks are always rattlers, copper heads, and water moccasins, and the waters draw wild ducks and any number of other wood creatures to drink and feed in and near Hillabahatchee's waters.

These plants and animals, which still thrive in this region of west Georgia where "progress" has been slow to arrive, have graced the Hillabahatchee locale for generations of human activity.

They were no doubt encountered by Mayhayley's grandparents as they made their first journey into Heard County in 1858. And they were all present as the family crossed that bridge.

As my brother tells it, the father pointed and recalled that he had learned to swim, thirty years before, in a deep swimming hole formed in the Hillabahatchee. In the midst of his story, he spotted Mayhayley in the road ahead. She was trudging uphill in the road's deep ruts. She was alone. No Sallie. No dogs were following her. So he tapped the car horn to get her attention, stopped the car, and offered her a ride.

She peered in the window and after she recognized him as a young man she had known all his life, she accepted the ride. After seeing the two boys in the back, Mayhayley sat down in the front seat with the little girl who was thus wedged between her father and Mayhayley.

The car moved off and continued climbing the hill as Mayhayley began to talk. "Now, Dewey, don't you worry about yourself and these children. You will get along all right. You've always been interested in getting ahead." She recounted parts of his life that she knew — stories of his parents, his grandparents, and his secret marriage that she had divulged in her newspaper column long ago.

She turned again to look at the two little boys sitting in the cavernous back seat, and said, "Dewey, those two boys will grow up, go to law school, and be lawyers like me." Then she picked up the little girl, pulled her on her lap, held her close, and said, "And this one, when she grows up, she'll do something about ME."

One of the boys became a lawyer; the other one graduated from law school, though he never practiced.

I am the little girl.

This book is the "something" I have done about Amanda Mayhayley Lancaster, "The Oracle of the Ages." To this fabulous, fascinating woman, I have given much of my time and near manic attention. This book will not end my relationship or my fascination with her. It certainly does not begin to explain her, fully. That, I think, is impossible. Instead, I remain only one of the many, many other people whose lives were touched by Mayhayley's mystique.

I accept and embrace her mystery, her enigma, her memory.

Appendix 1

Chronology of Mayhaley Lancaster

10/18/1875 Amanda Mayhayley Lancaster born.

9/10/1879 Sister Sallie born.

1892 AML first shows evidence of second sight—*Atlanta Journal*.

4/20/1894 Prof. E. E. Lewis closes school at Frolona, awards academic medal to AML (19 years old).

10/11/1895 AML opens 1st bank account at Citizens Bank, Carrollton, Georgia.

1896 AML advertises "A Horse Swap" meeting to be held at her house. "Bring all stock, goods, and 'indifferent.'"

9/6/1897 AML teaches school in Red Oak, Ga.; group photograph taken.

1899-1907 AML teaches school in Fair Falls, Alabama, Riverside, Fairview, and Rockalo, Georgia.

1908 AML begins to write weekly news column for Heard County newspaper *News and Banner* (N&B), opposes Populist movement, discusses need for knowledge and expounds on value of education. Writes "County needs railroad, cotton mills, wool factory, canning plant."

1908 AML advertises that she is agent for Memorial cards (N&B).

1907 AML pledges support for Carrollton A & M school (N&B).

1908 AML's sister Lucy dies. Sister Sallie "goes to Texas to make music for her uncle" (N&B).

2/24/1909 AML writes "brother Charles William Lewis Lancaster dies in Boswell, Oklahoma"(N&B) Tombstone reads: 2/4/1910.

6/4/1909 AML "thinking about moving to Franklin."

6/11/1909 "AML visiting in Carrollton and Atlanta for a couple of weeks" (N&B).

8/13/1909 "AML is working with Judge A. D. Freeman" (reading law) (N&B).

12/24/1909 AML teaches art at Macedonia Meeting House, Walnut Hill.

11/25/1910 "Georgia's and the World's Oracle, Miss A. Mayhayley Lancaster, since touring a great many cities and doing some of the best work in education will be stationed at her home near Walnut Hill, but will be at the home of Mrs. Louisa Alsabrooks at Crain next week for four days." (N&B). Sallie teaches music in Carrollton, Georgia, and marries Carl Mitchell.

2/10/1911 "AML will go February 2nd to the Atlanta Law School and will be admitted for the purpose of pleading law. Success to her as she is among the famous and talented Georgians and one of whom Heard County is truly proud" (N&B).

3/3/1911   AML defends Mrs. Lou Davis in her court case; refers to self as "the very good Heard County attorney" (N&B).

12/12/1911 "A man with a perpendicular line down his neck is a killer" (N&B).

12/12/1911 "Miss A. Mayhayley Lancaster represented the American Bar Association in the courtroom of Judge Alva Dean Freeman" (N&B).

4/26/1913 Mary Phagan murdered in Atlanta Pencil Factory; Leo Frank charged with murder. AML involved in trial of Frank. AML "is the very good Heard County attorney" (N&B).

1/23/1914 Little Johnnie Mitchell born to Sallie and Carl Mitchell.

8/16/1915 Leo Frank lynched in Marietta, Georgia. Mayhayley devastated.

1916   AML buys herself "a fine horse" N&B.

1916   Georgia allows women to practice law.

10/11/1917 AML's mentor, Judge Alva Dean Freeman dies in Newnan.

1/7/1919   AML's father buys a "new range and rubber-tired buggy for self and wife" (N&B).

2/10/1919 AML's father dies, "falls out of a chair, dead" (N&B).

10/5/1920 AML buys Lancaster home place.

8/1920   Women granted suffrage in U.S. AML writes that "the ladies must register to vote" (N&B).

8/25/1922 AML qualifies for election to Georgia Senate Seat.

9/15/1922 AML loses election to Judge Frank Loftin.

1923   "AML attending court in Atlanta, Newnan, Carrollton Won all cases" (N&B).

4/12/1925 AML buys lot and house in Franklin.

7/27/1926 AML qualifies for election to Georgia House Seat.

9/12/1926 AML loses election to J. Earl Faver.

7/27/1928 AML qualifies for election to Georgia Senate Seat, identifies self as "Heard County Attorney and Oracle."

9/12/1928 AML loses election to Dr. C.M. Mickle.

1928   AML buys lot in Franklin from C. Lester.

2/26/1929 Insurance company letter written concerning AML failure to pay.

1929   AML farming; delivers 14-inch ear of corn to N&B publisher.

8/24/1930 "Foretelling Death with Cards", full-page article about AML; Atlanta Journal article names person who knows victim of death prophecy.

1930   AML buys another store and dwelling in Franklin.

12/2/1930 AML buys 146 acres in Coweta County for $11.27 at Fi fa sale.

1932   AML buys 50 acres from J.P. Noles.

2/10/1933 AML lends money to neighbors.

1933   AML buying and selling mules and accepting cotton for collateral.

3/5/1934 AML buys 50 acres from J.G. Bledsoe, et al.

7/13/1934 "Ladies Beaten, Robbed Near Walnut Hill on Monday Night Last" (N&B).

3/1/1935 AML's mother dies.

12/3/1935 AML buys land from C.I. Carr.

9/22/37 AML buys 50 acres and mother's home place (Thaxton property).

9/22/37 AML buys 50 acres "stray land" in 12th district.

4/5/38 AML buys 100 acres and half interest in Lancaster Mill and mill shoals.

6/8/38 AML buys 23 acres north of Macedonia Church.

1/19/42 AML buys 100 acres from W. F. Gilbert, et al.

3/201944 AML involved in sicknesses from arsenic well-poisoning. Four die.

4/7/1948 John Wallace goes to see AML about lost cows.

6/11/1948 AML and Sallie at Coweta County Courthouse for Wallace trial.

6/14/1948 AML testifies at John Wallace trial, attracts media attention "Not since the 17th century has the testimony of a witch been allowed in a court of law," says A. L. Henson, defendant's attorney.

6/17/48 AML featured in *Atlanta Journal* article by Hugh Parks.

6/18/1948 John Wallace found guilty of murder.

6/20/1948 AML featured in *Atlanta Constitution* article by Celestine Sibley.

7/12/1948 AML featured in another *Atlanta Constitution* article by Sibley.

7/28/1948 AML has another robbery at home.

7/20/1948 AML money taken to Franklin bank by law officials.

7/30/1948 Four men apprehended in Arizona; plead guilty to robbing AML.

12/26/1948 AML predicts Peace and Early Spring for Newnan. *Atlanta Journal.*

2/16/1949 AML predicts "Newnan to be wiped off the map," *Newnan Times.*

2/17/1949 AML denies tornado destruction prediction of Newnan while City prepares for evacuation and Georgia Legislature votes funds for impending disaster.

4/12/1949 AML tells Anniston woman to search "at the end of porch and finds diamond ring."

11/3/1949 *Atlanta Constitution*: AML "tells where loves are true, finds lost jewelry, dogs or husbands."

1/11/1950 AML "locates wallet with $300" *Carrollton* (Georgia) *Times.*

5/17/1950 U.S. IRS levies tax lien on AML bank accounts for failure to pay taxes.

11/3/1950 John Wallace electrocuted for Turner murder.

2/14/1951 Funeral of John T. Chatman; body found by AML description.

2/1/1952 AML hospitalized in Carrollton, suffering pneumonia, etc.

3/12/1952 "Mayhayley not dead," reports Celestine Sibley.

3/16/1952 Mayhayley sick and hospitalized in Carrollton.

8/25/1952 Lancaster log house burns.

11/21/1952 Sallie lives in Roanoke with Johnnie; questions Lancaster home place ownership, letter from Carroll County Solicitor Earl Staples answers complaint.

12/7/1952 Sallie and Johnnie and family moved back to Heard County.

12/7/1952 Family members apply for guardianship of AML.

12/11/1952 AML deeds Bledsoe place to Johnnie Mitchell, Sallie's son.

1/23/1954 AML lunacy hearing held. Heard County Probate Court recommends commitment. LaGrange attorney Luther Wyatt and Franklin attorney Frank Gearreld represent family; Lamar Knight of Carrollton represents AML.

1/25/1954 AML withdraws $32,000 from bank for construction of new house.

1/25/1954 Judge Boykin enjoins Probate Court for AML commitment.

1/25/1954 AML writes secret will; leaves most to Sallie.

4/15/1954 AML moves into new house; has house warming celebration.

4/25/1954 AML featured in Columbus, Georgia, *Ledger-Enquirer.*

5/22/1955 AML dies; no autopsy performed.

5/24/1955 AML funeral: Caney Head Methodist Church, 3:00 PM.

5/26/1955 AML's will filed in Heard County Courthouse.

6/15/1955 AML will contested by some family members. In contest, family estimates her estate at $200,000.

7/14/1955 AML's death is *Atlanta Constitution* discussed by Celestine Sibley.

8/5/1955 AML estate contest answered.

3/14/1956 AML deposition of Dr. J.B. Wortham entered, "She was brilliant."

1957 AML's estate settled.

1/17/62 Johnnie Mitchell dies.

11/21/63 Sallie admitted to Central State Mental Hospital, Milledgeville, Georgia.

10/14/64 Sallie dies at Milledgeville.

8/30/1973 AML grave partially destroyed. "She was a former State Legislator," *Atlanta Constitution.*

1976 Margaret Anne Barnes's book,"Murder in Coweta County" published by *Reader's Digest* and Pelican Publishing Company, Gretna, La. Reprinted 1983.

1980 Johnny Cash buys movie rights to "Murder in Coweta County."

2/15/1983 First CBS broadcast of film "Murder in Coweta County." June Carter Cash plays Mayhayley.

1995 "Murder in Coweta County" videocassettes made available by Goodtimes Videos.

Appendix 2

Transcript of Wallace Trial Testimony

On June 14, 1948, in the Coweta County Courthouse in Newnan, Georgia, Mayhayley Lancaster testified for the State in the trial of John Wallace for the murder of Wilson Turner. Judge Sam Boykin was presiding. Solicitor Luther Wyatt prosecuted and A.L. Henson was representing the defendant. Mayhaley's testimony was one of the high points in a trial that had captured widespread public attention.

BY THE COURT: Bring the jury in.
(jury returns to the box.)

BY THE COURT: Call your next witness.
  MISS MAYHAYLEY LANCASTER
having been first duly sworn for the State, testifies as follows:
(**Direct Examination by Solicitor Wyatt**)
Q. You are Miss Mayhayley Lancaster?
  A. Yes, sir.
Q. Where do you live, Miss Mayhayley?
  A. Heard County, Georgia. Franklin, Route 3.
Q. How far on the other side of Franklin from here do you live?
  A. Ten miles measured.

Q. Do you know the defendant on trial, John Wallace?
  A. Yes, sir.
Q. Has he been to your house this year?
  A. Yes, sir.
Q. How many different times?
  A. About three.
Q. About three?
  A. Yes, sir.
Q. Did you ever hear him on any occasion that he was there threaten to kill anybody?
  A. Yes, sir.
Q. Who did he threaten to kill?
  A. A man who I didn't know, said "Wilson Turner."
Q. Wilson Turner?

A. Yes, sir.

Q. Did you know Wilson Turner?

A. No, sir.

Q. What did he come to your house for?

A. Said he lost two cows, and bought them in South Carolina, and they cost him $3,200.

Q. I can't understand you.

A. He said he lost two cows, and he bought them in South Carolina, and they cost him $3,200, and they were gone, and he wanted me to tell him where he could find the cows, said one was a milker and the other one was dry, and I said, "Turner." I said, "Carrollton, Georgia, it was in a pasture up there, carried there on a truck, and there was some paint or something put about the truck to keep down identification, and the truck that hauled the cows—," and he informed me he was going to Carrollton that night, and said if he found the cow and Turner he was going to kill him. I said, "Don't say that. That is a violation of the law, somebody was to meet you in the road and threatened a life like that, it would be a dead man down there." I said, "Don't say that."

Q. He came there twice about the cows?

A. Yes, sir.

Q. Did he ever come there about anybody else later?

A. Yes, something about finding a dead body somewhere.

Q. What is that?

A. Something about finding a dead body somewhere named Turner, and wanted to know would the body ever be located.

Q. Who wanted to know that?

A. Mr. Wallace.

Q. Mr. Wallace wanted to know?

A. Yes, sir.

Q. Did he tell you what body?

A. He said "Turner" and said Turner had lived about him from sometime, and he had a difference and said Turner moved away.

Q. And he wanted to know whether that body would be located or not?

A. Yes, sir. I told him it was in a well and green flies around it.

Q. Why was he coming to you and asking you that? What business are you engaged in?

A. He was having trouble. My business is fortune astrology and scientific reading.

Q. Scientific reading of the palm?

A. Yes, sir.

Q. Fortune telling, commonly referred to as fortune telling?

A. I don't call it fortune telling.

Q. People do call it that?

A. Same people do, but I don't.

Q. What did he say about the body, Miss Mayhayley?

A. He wanted to know where it would be located at.

Q. Did he tell you where it was?

A. No. He wanted to know himself.

Q. He wanted to know himself?

A. Yes, sir.

Q. Did he mention a well while he was talking to you?

A. I did to him, and told him there was some nails and green flies there, and they were taking the body out and putting it on a horse's back off of the farm where it was at, and muddied it somewhat so it would not be identified or fingerprints found on the horse.

At this point, Solicitor Wyatt returned to his seat and Atlanta attorney A. L. Henson addressed the witness chair for cross examination.

Cross Examination:

Q. I didn't get your name awhile ago.

A. Well, I would not especially care for my name to get in politics any more.

Q. You think it was in politics?

Judge Shirley Boykin addressed Mayhayley and orders:

BY THE COURT: Go ahead and give him your name.

A. It is M-A-Y-H-A-Y-L-E-Y.

Q. H-A-Y-L-E-Y?

A. L-A-N-C-A-S-T-E-R

Q. Caster?

A. Lancaster. It is an English name.

Q. Lancaster. Now you are what folks call a fortune teller?

A. I don't like that. I don't care for that so much.

Q. I know you don't but us folks that don't know the scientific name, we have to call it that

A. Really, I am called an oracle of the ages.

Q. A what?

A. An oracle of the ages.

Q. An oracle of the ages?

A. Yes, sir.

Q. Are you an oracle of the ages?

A. Yes. We were born that way. We were not made like school teachers.

Q. You were born that way, and you have been an oracle of the ages ever since you were born?

A. Yes.

Q. And you knew exactly where Turner's body was didn't you?

A. Well, I didn't see it.

Q. I know, but you knew?

A. I told the man where it was at.

Q. You don't have to see anything to know where it is or what it is, do you?

A. Well —

Q. Now an oracle of the ages can tell these things just in mind, just out of a clean atmosphere?

A. I don't know so much about that.

Q. You did that didn't you?

A. Well —

Q. You told right where the man was just by closing your eyes and letting a vision come to you?

A. No, I didn't close my eyes. I kept my eyes open.

Q. You kept your eyes open?

A. Yes, sir.

Q. But you did have to have a vision come to

you?

A. No, not so much.

Q. Well now, just how does the mind of an oracle of the ages work?

A. Well —

Q. How do you know all these things?

A. The wise forseeth and hideth himself.

Q. And that is how you got all this information? You are just the wise forseeth, and hideth the information? Is that what an oracle of the ages does?

A. I do many things. I buy oxen and mules.

Q. Now did these officers come to you to get their information?

A. Considerably few of them.

Q. And the information that they have got here they got it from you?

A. I don't know about that.

Q. What?

A. I don't know about that.

Q. How many of them went to you? Did Mr. Goldberg come to you to find out just exactly what the truth of it was?

A. I would not know Mr. Goldberg.

Q. This handsome young gentleman over here, did he come to find out the whole story about this?

A. There was some men over there. I would not testify an oath that was him.

Q. Look at him. Did he come?

A. I remember seeing him, but I don't remember talking with him.

Q. He came and got from you the information about this case?

A. Well, there was one man named Hancock, but I do not know where he come from.

Q. Mr. Hancock?

A. And another man.

Q. He is an investigator in this case.

A. Another man.

Q. And he got his information from you?

A. — By the name of—He was a deputy sheriff sometime, and he now lives in LaGrange.

Q. Look at this gentleman twirling the hat before you. Did he come and get his information from you?

A. Well, I would not say, because there is so many of them, Mister. I could not keep up with them.

Q. Look at him good. How many times did he come to find out about this affair?

A. Well, I didn't keep up with it this time.

Q. You didn't keep up with it?

A. No, sir.

Q. Do you know the prosecuting attorney over here?

A. Yes, very well.

Q. How many times did he come.

A. Not at all.

Q. You mean he didn't come to see you to get this information?

A. No.

Q. Well, you had it all didn't you?

A. Had a what?

Q. The information

A. I don't think so. I think some they have not got yet.

Q. What?

A. I don't think so. I think there is some they have not got yet.

Q. You mean there is some information you have got yet, and you are an oracle of the ages?

A. Well, you are not paying me to tell you.

Q. Well, they are going to pay you the witness fees.

A. I am not dunning them.

Q. If I was to pay you to tell me, could you tell?

A. No, I would not do that.

Q. You would not?

A. No.

Q. Well, you know though, don't you?

A. Well, you are not examining my brains.

Q. I am not.

A No.

Q. You are not going to tell me all you know, are you?

A. Well, I will tell you what I do know, a reasonable amount.

Q. Are you going to tell this jury all you know?

A. No.

Q. You are not?

A. I know things I would not tell them.

Q. You don't think they know what they do?

A. On the square, I would not tell.

Q. Would not even tell this jury? All right now, how many cows did this man Turner steal from Mr. Wallace?

A. Two.

Q. Just two. How about the four they found over in Carroll County? Did you know the cows were over there?

A. I didn't know anything about it.

Q. Do you mean to tell this jury that you didn't know where these cows were tied?

A. Well, this man told me that he bought the cows in South Carolina.

Q. I didn't ask you that, I asked you this: Do you mean to tell this jury that you didn't know there was four cows tied out over here in Carroll County?

A. I never saw the cows in my life.

Q. You don't have to see anything to know it, being an oracle, do you? You didn't see these green flies circling around this man's body in the well?

A. I told him there was some there.

Q. I know you did, but you didn't see them, did you?

A. Well, the wise man forseeth evil and hideth himself.

Q. What I mean to say, did you see the flies with your natural eyes, the one you are looking at me with?

A. I have an artificial left eye.

Q. The artificial eye then, did you see the flies flying around the body?

A. I didn't go to the well.

Q. How do you know they were there?

A.   Well, I saw very well.

Q.   What?

A.   I saw very well that the body was put in a well and the green flies was swarming around there, and a hand full of nails laying in there.

Q.   You saw that?

A.   Not down there I didn't.

Q.   Where did you see it?

A.   Well, astrology is a science that treats the stars.

Q.   I see.

A.   Presented to me through the stars.

Q.   Now tell the jury just how it got to you through the stars.

A.   Well, the jury is examining a murder case and not the stars.

Q.   I didn't ask you that. I asked you to tell the jury how the information of this well and these flies happened to get to you through the stars. Just tell them how you saw it You know what it is to take an oath and swear the truth.

A.   I have sworn a good many times.

Q.   You know what it means to take an oath don't you? Just answer yes or no.

A.   I am not going to tell the Court or anybody else I saw them flies with my natural eyes.

Q.   Well now how did you see them? Now you say you didn't see them with your natural eyes. Have you got another pair of eyes you can see them things?

A.   Crawfishes eyes are in their tail, and mine is in my head.

Q.   You must have some where the crawfish's eyes are, because you say you didn't see it with the ones in your head. Tell the jury what pair of eyes you did see this man in the well with.

A.   I told you I only had one eye.

Q.   Just one eye. Well, you didn't see the flies with that eye did you?

A.   I told you I didn't see the flies at all, because I was not in that Country. I was back up here at home.

Q.   You were back up at home, and never did go down there in your life ever?

A.   Yes. I have been in that country.

Q   You never did go to this well?

A.   I didn't have any business there.

Q.   You never did go there did you?

A.   Not to that well, I didn't.

Q.   Yet you told Mr. Wallace that the man's body was in it, didn't you?

A.   Well, he knew what they put in there.

Q.   I didn't ask you. Did you tell him that? Did you tell him that the man's body was in the well and that green flies were there?

A.   And they were going to move it.

Q.   May I ask you this question: Has the all wise God given you more wisdom than the officers that investigated this case?

A.   My share.

Q.   He has? And that is what you base your information on, that extra wisdom that God gave you but didn't give these offfcers?

A.   No. I feel my importance.

Q.   What?

A.   I feel my importance.

Q. You feel your importance?

A. Yes.

Q. Are you more important than these officers?

A. Well, if there is anything in the truthful line according to the laws of the State, where I was born and raised, I am so.

Q. According to the laws of the State where you were born and raised?

A. According to the law.

Q. Did you say you were more important or less?

A. More.

Q. You are more important. The reason you are more important is because you can know things without seeing them, hearing them, or feeling them, isn't it?

A. I have the advantage of you. You can't do it.

Q. I know, but you can, can't you?

A. I do do it.

Q. And that is the information that you gave these boys about this case, was it not?

A. Well, they found what they were hunting.

Q. I see, and when they did, just like you told them?

A. They said they did.

Q. Just like you told them?

A. They said they did.

Q. They found it all true. Now you told Mr. Wallace that a cow was over in county?

A. Carroll County.

Q. And he went over there, and sure enough he found it.

A. He said he did.

Q. And now did you hear Mr. Turner — Did you tell Mr. Wallace about Turner being —

A. Yes, I told him about a man named Turner.

Q. You told him a man named Turner was out with a gun to threaten him didn't you?

A. I don't recall about that.

Q. Well, you knew that he was didn't you?

A. No. I didn't personally know Turner.

Q. What?

A. I just found his name in my own way.

Q. Found it in your own way?

A. And pointed it out to him.

Q. Now in your own way didn't you find him packing a gun to kill Mr. Wallace with because Mr. Wallace didn't want whiskey made on his farm?

A. No.

Q. You didn't? You didn't turn on that part of the switch did you, to connect with the stars?

A. The switch didn't have anything to do with it.

Q. Well now, just how do you find — how do you decide what you want to know? You don't have to see anything to know it, believe you said, feel it or hear it. How do you decide what you want to know, and what information you want, just automatically turn on?

A. The court don't care anything about it. It don't concern the case.

Q. Well, the Court does. The Court wants to

know how you can focus your information finder.

A.   It would not have any weight with the case.

Q.   Would not have any weight?

A.   No.

Q.   Haven't you said you are of a great deal more importance than these other folks?

A.   I would say so if it is my opinion.

SOLICITOR WYATT: I think it would be confined to the questions and answers brought out.

JUDGE BOYKIN: I think so. Confine it to evidence brought out by the State on Direct Examination.

MR. HENSON continued:

Q.   Do you read any newspapers?

A.   Sure.

Q.   Did you tell these newspaper reporters what to put in them?

A.   No.

Q.   How did they know if they didn't talk to you?

A.   I don't know how they knew.

Q.   You don't? Now Mr. Wallace was joking about killing somebody that was taking his cattle.

A.   No, he said he was going to do it.

Q.   Well, you knew what was going to happen. You can tell what is going to in the future, can't you?

A.   You ought to get me to tell you sometime and see how you come out.

Q.   Well, could you do it?

A.   I might.

Q.   Well, I want to know could you tell me what is going to happen in the future to me?

A.   You may get what Turner got.

JUDGE BOYKIN: Let's go to something else. The witness is excused.

The Will of A. Mayhayley Lancaster

Georgia, Heard County

I, A. Mayhayley Lancaster, a resident of State of Georgia, Heard County, being of sound and disposing mind and memory, and being imbued with the uncertainty of life, hereby revoke any previous wills, and declare this to be my Last Will and Testament.

Item 1

I desire and direct that my body be buried in a Christianlike manner suitable to my circumstances and condition in life at Caney Head Methodist Church in Heard County, Georgia.

Item 2

I desire and direct that all of my just debts be paid, including all taxes which shall be paid out of my estate without unnecessary delay by my Executors herein named and appointed.

Item 3

I desire to and do make the following spe-cial bequests: the sum of ONE HUNDRED ($100 00) DOLLARS [sic] to be paid to each of my sisters and brother, to-wit: Nancy C. Paschal, of Carrollton, Carroll County, Georgia: Mrs. Mary Arrington, of Carroll County, Georgia, Louise E. Cosper, of Jasper, Alabama, my sisters, and R. G. Lancaster, of Cullman, Alabama, my brother. Said sums to my sisters and brother to be in full of their interest in my estate.

Item 4

All the rest, residue and remainder of my estate, either personalty, realty or choses in action wherever the same may be located, or any interest I may have therein, I hereby will, bequeath and devise to my sister, Mrs. Sarah F. Hull, who has cared for me and lived with me throughout the many years, in fee simple, to all remainder of my property wherever the same may be located.

Item 5

I hereby name, appoint, and select my sister, Mrs. Sarah F. Hull, and Mr. Lamar Knight of Carollton, Georgia, as Executors of this my Last Will and Testament, or either of them as may qualify, and I fully authorize and empower my said Executors herein named to administer my estate without the intervention, or necessity of procuring order of any Court relative to the disposition, sale, or advertisements concerning the administration of my estate, relieving my said Executors from making bond, any returns to any court, or having any appraisements made. Said Executors are empowered to sell any part of all of my estate either at public or private sale, with or without advertisement, without procuring any order so to do, and to make good and sufficient conveyance to the purchaser, or purchasers, or to make any returns upon.

The signature portion of Mayhaley's will.

Index

A

Affiliated Lyceum Bureau of
America   61
American Bar Association   123
Anniston, Alabama   66
Arrington, Marvin   106, 109
Arrington, Mary
Lancaster   94, 101–111
death of   111
Atlanta Constitution   55, 84
Atlanta Journal   67, 120

B

Bank of Heard County   57, 124
Bankhead, Tallulah   63, 67–69, 69–70, 70–71
Barnes, Margaret Anne   48
Beavers, J. A.   48
Bledsoe, Charlie   97
Bledsoe, John   27, 103
Bledsoe, Virgil   53, 97
Bowers, R. L.   71
Bryan, Bud and Dessie   90
Bryan, Clara   86–100
death of   100
Bryan, James   129
Bryan, Lovic   86, 92–100

C

Caldwell, Herman   97
Caney Head Methodist
Church   72, 95, 97, 101, 104, 125

Cannon, Sarah. *See* Pearl, Minnie
Carmichael, A. B.   71
Carroll County Courthouse   65, 121
Carroll County Prison   57
Carrollton A&M   29
Caswell, Doyle   95
Chambers County, Alabama   53, 76
Chambers County Courthouse   121
Chattahoochee River   49, 131
Chesnut, G. Y.   71
Cosper, Albert   87–90
Cosper, Bertha   88–90
Cosper, Jim   89
Cosper, Tommie   87–90
Coweta County Courthouse   78, 80, 121
Coweta County, Georgia   48, 76

D

Disney, Walt   63
Dukes, Joe Will   71
Dunaway Gardens   60, 64, 70, 72, 125
Dunaway, Hettie Jane
(Sewell)   60–73
death of   73
first meeting with
Mayhayley   60
Dunaway, Marjorie   64, 66

F

Farmer, J. J., Jr.   71
Frank, Leo   103, 119
Franklin, Georgia   51, 114, 132
Freeman, Alva Dean   122
Front-Page Detective   71

G

Gearreld, Frank   114–127
death of   127
George, Ron (pseud-
onym)   136
Gladney, Ezra   50, 52, 52–53
Gordon Military School   76
Great Depression   62

H

Hardy, C. W.   71
Harris County, Georgia   85
Heard County, Georgia   44, 50, 64, 76, 78, 87, 97, 100, 114, 134
Hemmings, Willis   27–43
death of   43
first meeting with Mayhayley
Lancaster   29
Henson, A. L.   83
Hillabahatchee Creek   132
Hillin, Jim   49, 79
Holderness, Sid   65–66

J

James, Frank   51
James, Jesse   51

Jasper, Alabama 67, 70
Jennings, Alice Denton 77
John Wallace trial 48–50, 71, 78–85
Johnson, Edgar 48

K

Ku Klux Klan 117

L

LaGrange Daily News 56
LaGrange Graphic 117
Lancaster, Bennie 101
Lancaster, Charles W. L. 104, 106
Lancaster, Charlie 106
Lancaster, Lucy 98
Lancaster, Mahala (great-grandmother) 102
Lancaster, Mayhayley 34–43
  as fortune teller 32, 46–48, 56, 66, 69, 75, 76, 120, 132, 135
  as lawyer 122–124
  born with a caul 104
  dealing with John Wallace 76–77
  death of 72, 94–95, 108
  disputes with others 88–89, 124
  disputes with the family 102
  eccentricities of 90–92, 129–130
  first meeting with Willis Hemmings 29
  funeral of 97–100, 126
  getting robbed 50–53
  involved in politics 103, 116–119
  involved in the John Wallace trial 49, 71, 77–85
  losing her eye 44
  running numbers 39–41, 92
  suffering from ailments 87, 92–94, 107
  writing her weekly newspaper column 31
Lancaster, Sallie 33, 40, 49, 51, 80, 89, 93–100, 102, 105–111
  death of 128
Lancaster, Watson 103, 119
Lassiter, Homer 71
Lipford, Mort 55, 120
Loftin, Frank 114, 127

M

Meriwether County, Georgia 48, 76, 77
Mickle, Dr. C. M. 117
Mickle, Hugh 126
Mitchell, Evie Farmer 106, 128–139
  death of 139
Murder in Coweta County 48, 57
Murphy, Bud 56

N

Neely, W. C. 71
New Hope Baptist Church 135
Newby, C. E. 71
Newnan, Georgia 49, 62, 80, 114
Newnan Times-Herald 56
News and Banner 103, 119, 123, 132
Noles, Marvin 39, 41

O

Odom, Sam 97
Otwell, J.C. 44–57, 79
  death of 57

P

Paschal, Nancy 89
Pearl, Minnie 62
Persons, Lela 134
Phagan, Mary 103, 119
Plant, Willie 71
Potts, Lamar 71, 76, 78, 80
Pretty Boy Floyd 51
Prince, O. W. 71

R

Randolph County, Alabama 121
Ridley, Grady 135
Roanoke, Alabama 51, 130, 139
Roosevelt, Franklin 77, 118
Rural Electric 28

S

Sewell Production Company 62
Sewell, Wayne 60–73, 116
  as "Ziegfield of the South" 62
  death of 73
  first encounter with Mayhayley 64–66
Sibley, Celestine 104
Simms, John 64, 66
Simonton, Carl 119
Skinner, G. W. 56
Smith, Col. Willis 122
South, Rudy 51

Staples, Earl   106
Stewart, Lucile Long   67, 69
Strawbridge, Edwin   63
Strickland, Mozart   76
Stutts, Steve   98, 108

T

Talmadge, Eugene   118
Talmadge, Herman   118
Taylor, J. C.   117
The Jeffersonian   119
Troup County Court-
    house   121
Turner, Wilson   48, 49, 76, 78,
    82

V

Veal Baptist Church   105

W

Wallace, John   48–50, 75–85
    death of   85
    first encounter with
        Mayhayley   76
    trial of   41
Watson, Tom   119
Webster, Jordan (pseud-
    onym)   133
Wheeler, James (pseud-
    onym)   115–127
Whitlock, C. E.   71
Wyatt, Luther   49, 78, 82, 124,
    134

Y

Young Harris School   76

A 1980 photo of Mayhayley Lancaster's grave after it had been repaired from damage. The epitaph reads: "For Neither Did His Brethren Believe in Him. St. John, Seventh Chapter, Fifth Verse"